June 3, 2012

Embracing the
Refiner's Fire

Dearest Helen,
You have been such a comfort and support to Dale, to me, to our whole family, thru this journey through the valley of the shadow of death. Thank you for being there. Love, Guy

Embracing the
Refiner's Fire

Dale and Ruby Price
with Steve Van Atta

Goehner Publications
San Jose, CA

Copyright © 2011 by Dale and Ruby Price
Artwork by Elaine Roemen
Book design by Jaira Hill

The cover artwork, painted by Elaine Roemen, was a favorite of Dale's. It hangs in the Price home. Entitled "The Warrior," Dale chose this painting for the cover of this book as a metaphor for his fight against cancer and Christ's fight for us as His beloved children.

Printed in the United States of America

ISBN 9780983128519

Dedication

This book is dedicated to the glory of our Lord Jesus Christ, and to our sons, Josh and Matt, and our grandsons, Tyler, Cody, Noah, Logan, and Finly.

Amy's Garden by Elaine Roemen

List of Artwork

by Elaine Roemen

Contents

Foreword

The value of a life is measured more by its donation than its duration. And so it was and is with Dale and Ruby Price, whose life journey is captured in this gripping book.

As you step into this narrative, you will be drawn into a real life story that will captivate your heart, mind and soul. Through the excruciating pain of seeing a healthy, energetic and successful leader, supported by his loving and talented wife and family, all being ravaged by the hell of cancer, you will soon be engrossed in matters that transcend the plight of this human tragedy. You will be challenged to consider how cancer of the body does not necessarily spread to cancer of the soul! Discover how that happened for the Prices and could be true for you.

It matters not whether you are a seeker, cynic, or follower of Jesus, you will be drawn into this book. See the difference it makes to embrace Jesus as your personal Savior and then ask, "Given my personal circumstances, what should I do right now?" Quietly and deliberately, you will be challenged to embrace your God-inspired insights and answers. It doesn't matter where you are or have been, but only where you are going.

One of the reasons this book will captivate you is because it avoids the rehearsed platitudes of so many Christian books. It openly gives expression to the human realities of pain, fear, grief, and the like, while embracing a spiritual discovery process. In this context the Bible will come alive through the eyes of Dale, Ruby, their family, and the testimonies and tributes of myriads that crossed paths with them in life.

Truly God's preferred method of communicating His love, hope and message is embedding it within real people like Dale and Ruby, frail as they may be, and then watch it spread to others who encounter Jesus Christ for themselves.

Thank you Dale, Ruby, family and friends for sharing your story. The physical struggle and death of Dale Price, a choice servant of Christ, points the way to greater spiritual triumphs for each of us. For this wonderful gift, Dale and Ruby, we are eternally grateful.

Bob Kobielush
Colleague and friend
Former president,
Christian Camp and Conference Association

Acknowledgments

Special thanks to the many friends, family members, ministry partners and professional colleagues who were willing to be interviewed by co-author Steve Van Atta, or contributed written materials he used in the writing of the book.

The book could not have been completed without the creativity and hard work of Jaira Hill. A longtime and very close friend of the Prices, Jaira shaped the book's layout and graphic design; gathered notes from CaringBridge and other sources; and coordinated the selection and placement of art work.

Thanks, too, to Don Goehner and Goehner Publications, for providing project oversight to the book.

The Dale Price Memorial Fund provides partial and full scholarships for young people participating in the Canyonview Camp Christian-leadership programs Dale founded. Contributions can be sent to Canyonview Camp, P.O. Box 128, Silverton, OR 97381.

Preface

When my beloved husband, Dale Price, Executive Director of Canyonview Camp, was diagnosed with Stage 3B lung cancer in August 2008, waves of grief shattered life as we knew it. *Embracing the Refiner's Fire* is the story of our journey with the Great Shepherd into the valley of the shadow of death.

Dale's story is one of God's mercy and grace, as well as how the loving Master Craftsman's refining fire created a work that reflected His glory.

One of the great lessons we learned on this journey was how to fully abide in Christ, recognizing the Lord's presence in every moment of our lives. Although we could not see around the corner to know God's future for us, we trusted in His leading and chose each day to abide in His love. We had confidence that His plans were good; abiding was and is the hardest thing that we have ever done.

Dale daily demonstrated incredible courage. During our nearly three year walk with cancer, Dale and I found that looking back could bring regrets; looking forward, fear; the only place where we could find peace and joy was in the present. The key ingredients of this altered life-view included both a renewed sense of appreciation for what is, and a sharper vision for what is truly important.

As he walked through the valley of the shadow of death, Dale discovered that his transparency allowed people to see him, a respected and loved Christian leader, broken and on his knees before God. *Embracing the Refiner's Fire* shows how God used Dale's cancer to bring him into an even closer relationship with his Lord. That closeness 'qualified' him to minister more deeply to those who were suffering.

I have been reading and re-reading this tattered piece of

paper I've been carrying around in my purse, in which Dale wrote:

"I have come to realize in all of these things that our compre-hension of our time on earth is an illusion. The moment in which we live is all we have and it is where God's will is realized. It is in the present now that we learn to abide, to trust, to hope, to love, to be filled with His peace and joy.

"I pray that you will find God's perfect peace as you abide in His love. It is the only place where I have found joy in the midst of what may be terminal for me. We may all be Home sooner than expected."

Dale lost his Herculean battle with cancer in the early hours of April 16th, 2011. Dale lived and died, glorifying his Savior.

Ruby Price

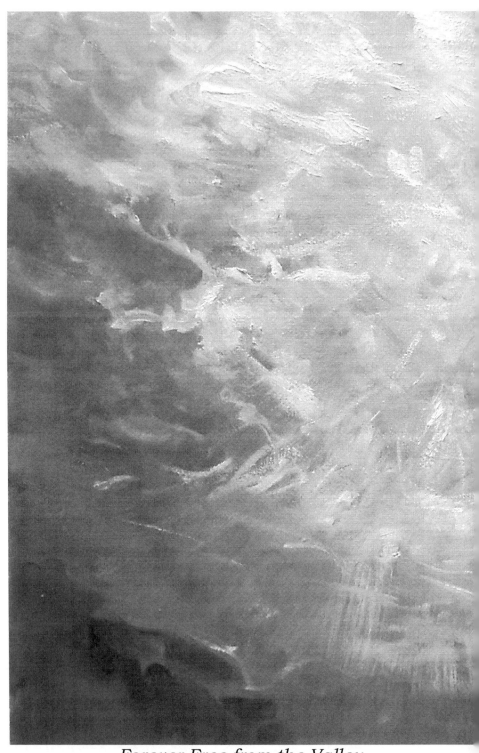

Forever Free from the Valley

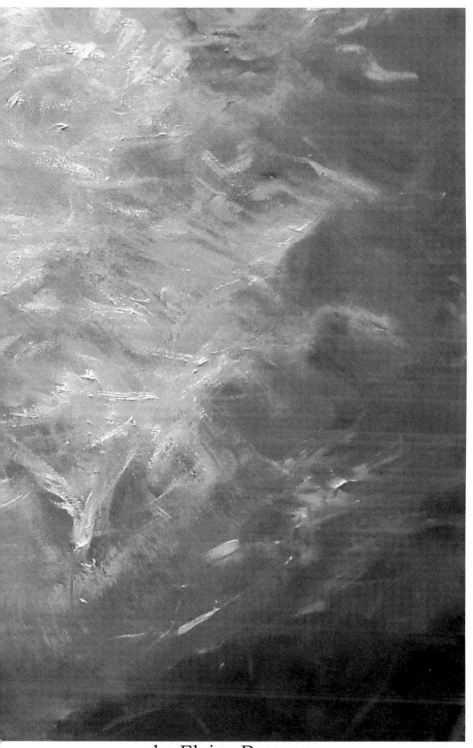

by Elaine Roemen

Chapter 1

Unexpected News, Uncertain Journey

"I ask Him, 'Why?' Not in anger or resistance or self-pity, but because I want to understand.

"More than just gaining knowledge about my health and medical issues, I want to understand the Lord's new plan for me. I'm still in shock, but I know I'm embarking on a new journey.

"And I'm not going alone!"

"What would I do if I had been given your diagnosis? I'd buy some flip flops, grab my wife, head for Hawaii and enjoy the six months before I died."

Dale Price always prized honesty in others, but when he was diagnosed with advanced lung cancer on August 20, 2008, his doctor's truth-telling was almost too much to bear.

Dale's condition was beyond "not so good" or "challenging." What had been questions about a nagging cough and occasional discomfort now had a name.

Cancer.

Just seeing the word can be scary. The disease, regardless of its proximity to us, terrifies us. Cancer is part of our shared human experience and the landscape of our health concerns. How much do we think about cancer? Every day, people Google the word "cancer" more than 1 million times.

The toll is heartbreaking. New cancer cases in the U.S. each year: 1.5 million. Deaths annually from cancer: 570,000. The Number 1 killer among cancer types: lung cancer. And that's just the physical impact. For many, living with cancer or loving someone who has cancer brings pain as wrenching as the disease itself.

Dale and Ruby Price went from knowing the obvious (everyone dies), to observing the specifics (some people die from cancer), to becoming the victim (Dale has cancer and probably won't live long). The hypothetical became their reality. Their question went from What if? to What now?

Symptoms and signs

When someone who appears to be in excellent health begins to show signs to the contrary, we often doubt our perceptions, not their medical condition. "No, I'm just imagining it. He's in such great shape. I'm sure it's nothing. Besides, it's really none of my business."

The trouble was that the cough Dale had had on and off for two years was getting worse, some people thought, not better.

> *He had been coughing for a long time and we wondered what it was. He was a powerful man, but wasn't acting strong. Plus, he was crabby sometimes, a first for him in the 25 years I'd known him.*
>
> *In 2007 I started getting concerned. The next year, he looked even more exhausted and was coughing up blood. I didn't even consider the problem to be cancer, but we insisted that he get an appointment with the doctor.*

Despite signs of health troubles, Dale and Ruby were not about to slow down, not when family adventures and ministry opportunities kept coming their way. During the summer of 2008 they headed for the Republic of Czech where Dale, among other activities, officiated at his niece's wedding. They also spent time sightseeing and hiking in Austria.

BECAUSE MY coughing wouldn't stop and Ruby insisted that I get it checked, I went in for an exam and x-rays during our time in Europe. They ruled out TB and pneumonia, but had no answers about what was going on in my chest. When we returned from our trip, I made an appointment with our local doctor, who ordered a CAT scan.

I pray that the test results will reveal the reason for my persistent cough and headaches. The CAT scan targeted my lungs and my sinuses, but I am not worried.

After the test, I went with the guys to take down the Butte Creek camp. On my way back I called the doctor's

office, offering to pick up any medication the CAT scan indicated I would need to get rid of the cough. Instead, I heard,
"He wants to see you in his office tomorrow."

The nurse's words and tone of voice sounded ominous;
it turned out that today would be our last, blessed day of
ignorance. Tomorrow will change the rest of my life. I expressed my concerns to my fellow elders and we prayed.

"I just couldn't believe it"

I WILL never forget this day, Wednesday, August 20,
2008. I gather with friends at O'Brien's restaurant for prayer
and Bible study, unsettled and anxious about my doctor appointment that afternoon.

Sitting in the doctor's office, waiting for him to arrive, I
had time to wonder what the test had revealed that re-
quired this urgent visit. And I had time to pray again for
God's peace.

As Dr. L. came in, I asked him, "How are you doing?"

"Terrible."

"Because of you or because of me?"

"Because of you. The good news is that your sinuses are
clear."

"And?"

"You have lung cancer."

His words hit hard, boring into my brain and clouding my
vision. A second appointment, with a pulmonologist, has
already been scheduled for Friday. The rest of the day and
evening are a blur.

I'm afraid, but also have faith in God. Conflicting and
complex feelings race through my heart and mind; despair
battles hope.

When I first heard the diagnosis, shock waves tore
through me. Denial was the very first reaction. I'm as fit as

I've been in years. It's just a cough. I bike, run, work hard at the camp, hike. I feel alone, but at the same time I experience God's strong, comforting presence. He is still with me; He is still in control of that which I cannot control.

I ask Him, "Why?" Not in anger or resistance or self-pity, but because I want to understand. More than just gaining knowledge about my health and medical issues, I want to understand the Lord's new plan for me. I'm still in shock, but I know I'm embarking on a new journey. And I'm not going alone!

I told my older son, Josh, the news and on Thursday evening I talked with my younger son Matt. (By God's grace he came out of the wilderness early – blown out by a storm – and is with me when I need him most.) My sons are such a blessing, simultaneously strong and tender in all they do. I found out later that they cried and prayed together for me.

I called Ruby and asked her to come home from Port Orford. "We need to be together this weekend." I tell her about the lung-cancer diagnosis, but the rest of the information and feelings and fears are too hard to speak to her over the phone. Listening to her, I'm starting to feel some of the deep grief others will feel.

When describing a time of trauma, crisis or other life-changing event, we often begin with words like, "I'll never forget where I was when…" For some, it's the JFK assassination; for others, their conversion to Christ; some recall the D-Day invasion, or when man first walked on the moon.

For others, including Ruby, it was when they found out Dale Price had lung cancer.

Today, August 22, 2008, life changed forever. My life, my husband's life, our kids' lives, the lives of hundreds

– maybe thousands – of people around the globe.

After working very hard in my third year as superintendent of the Port Orford-Langlois School District, everything was ready to kick off the 2008-09 school year. As I finished up my preparations, I got a call from my husband, Dale.

While it was odd that he should call and suggest I drive the 4½ hours home that weekend – we had already agreed that he would drive down this weekend - what was really strange was what I heard in the background during Dale's call. Our son, Matt, was telling his dad, "You have to tell Mom. Now."

Then I heard the life-changing words as Dale whispered, "You need to come home because the doctor is 99 percent sure I have lung cancer."

I felt myself tumbling into a state of shock. It couldn't be lung cancer! Pneumonia maybe, but lifelong nonsmokers like Dale don't get lung cancer.

Within 45 minutes I was on my way, driving north on Highway 101. The lines on the road were hard to see through the tears. Matt called while I was driving, saying, "Mom, I love you. Do you want me to drive down and get you?" My eyes and face flooded with tears and gratitude for his love. I knew I could make it home, though it took longer than usual as I had to stop several times when the sobs and tears overcame my ability to drive.

As I drove into the driveway of our cozy home where we had lived for more than 30 years, Dale was waiting on the steps to greet me. For a fleeting moment it all seemed like a bad dream, not part of our real lives. This isn't an emergency trip home because my husband's been diagnosed with cancer, it's just one of the thousands of times I've come home, eager to be in the arms of the man I've loved for nearly 40 years. But the look on his face told me instantly that our lives had, indeed, changed forever. That night we

"In meekness, I want to submit to the Master's will because I trust God, not because I understand what His will might be. Am I facing death in just a few months? Miraculous healing? A lifetime of sickness? I don't know, but He does."

talked late, until there were no more words to say and we just held each other tight.

Matt and I insisted that Dad get an appointment to find out about the coughing. But they found spots on his lungs when they ran the CAT scan. This is not good. A second, more comprehensive appointment was ordered, including a biopsy.

Hearing those words - "Your dad has, probably, only six months to live." - absolutely devastated us.

ఞఞఞ

When Ruby told me the news I couldn't believe it. At first I thought she was talking about someone else, not Dale. I dropped to the floor, crying, praying, asking God for help. There was no sleep in our home that night.

I'd known for quite awhile that something was wrong. Now, sadly, I knew what it was. Cancer? Oh, no. Getting the news felt like being pushed off a cliff, falling but never hitting the bottom. He only has only six months to live? This can't be happening.

ఞఞఞ

When Dale told us he'd gone to the doctor and

they had found a tumor, I was very surprised. But I thought, well, they can get a tumor out. He'll be OK. When the complete test results arrived, they contained the worst possible news. It wasn't just a tumor. He had Stage-4 lung cancer. With the advanced condition of Dale's cancer and lung cancer's aggressive nature of attack, the doctors predicted he would be dead in less than a year.

I thought, this is wrong. He's so amazing, so active, so important to so many people. It was almost like he had died already. Those moments, those days, were gut-wrenching. We started praying, hard. I wasn't upset with God, but I pleaded with Him, "Please don't take away this man from our lives, from the kids at camp… from the world!"

∽∽∽

When Dale called to tell me of his diagnosis, it was more than hard to believe. A lifelong non-smoker could get the dread disease associated with the use of tobacco? My brother in the Lord, the same age as me, was facing imminent death? My husband and I felt a gripping agony in our bodies when we received the call from Dale. We knew he had been coughing for the last few months and felt something was wrong, but thought it might be pneumonia. Or tuberculosis, at the very worst. We were devastated and in tears at the news.

∽∽∽

I'd only known Dale for a few months before his diagnosis, but I insisted that he not meet with his doctor alone. We went to the hospital together that day and prayed before the doctor delivered the stunning report. Dale didn't know how to tell his family, when to tell them, or how much to tell them. I was concerned for him, but unsure about the best way to help.

Some in our church family were completely paralyzed by the news. "Cancer? No way, not Dale Price! He's in such good shape, so healthy." A number of people were in denial for days, even weeks. When the Canyonview Camp staff found out, there were more tears, more questions, more prayer.

Sunday, August 24, 2008

"The Spirit of the Lord shall rest upon Him, the spirit of wisdom and understanding, the Spirit of counsel and might, the Spirit of knowledge and of the fear of the Lord." Isaiah 11:2

TODAY WAS a day when we needed God's wisdom, the kind that only comes from the Spirit of the Lord. At the Sunday school class I had a chance to share briefly about our situation. Ruby and I decided we should let the entire church body know what is going on.

Why is it important to share this news publicly? Because this is our spiritual family. Our sons had grown up here and I'd been interim pastor. I'd known these people for 30 years. Our lives, families, activities and ministries were deeply and fruitfully intertwined.

So at the conclusion of the service, Ruby and I made a clear and complete explanation about the cancer, the options available to us, and our immediate needs. That was followed by an amazing outpouring of love, prayer, hope, concern, and comfort. The body of Christ was so precious to us that morning, caring for and supporting us in ways we'd cherish and soon rely on to an even greater degree.

"Afflicted...but not crushed"

"WE ARE AFFLICTED IN EVERY WAY, BUT NOT CRUSHED; PERPLEXED, BUT NOT DESPAIRING; PERSECUTED, BUT NOT FORSAKEN; STRUCK DOWN, BUT NOT DESTROYED; ALWAYS CARRYING ABOUT IN THE BODY THE DYING OF JESUS, SO THAT THE LIFE OF JESUS ALSO MAY BE MANIFESTED IN OUR BODY." 2 CORINTHIANS 4:8-10

I grieved so much after the diagnosis. We knew he would keep working, remaining active and strong to the end. My dad was tireless, accomplishing much more than anyone I knew. Cancer might slow him down but it wouldn't stop him. He was always so committed to keeping first things first, especially when it came to family. My dad spent lots of time with us guys, our wives and the grandkids.

One of our biggest hurts came with knowing that we'd lose our future with him, realizing Grandpa probably wouldn't be around for his grandkids' growing-up years. Facing the fact that I wouldn't always be able to just pick up the phone and call him or catch up with him as he worked on a project at camp. The days of asking him, "Hey, Dad, how did you handle this situation?" were numbered.

అల్లఅల్ల

When I think about my dad - the incredible father he's been for us, the wonderful grandfather he's been for the kids and the awesome husband he's been for my mom - I must face the truth: our days together are way shorter than we ever thought they'd be.

"BLESSED ARE THE MEEK, FOR THEY SHALL INHERIT THE LAND." MATTHEW 5:5 (NIV)

I AM in a place of great meekness. The diagnosis is confirmed beyond any shadow of doubt. My cancer is not subject to my control and understanding, and I don't know the prognosis for success in my cancer battle.

In meekness, I want to submit to the Master's will because I trust God, not because I understand what His will might be. Am I facing death in just a few months? Miraculous healing? A lifetime of sickness? I don't know, but He does. And that's enough for me today.

Ruby and I awoke together, a simple pleasure that provided us with great comfort. We get up, walk and talk. There is so much to say, but even more that is left unsaid. That's OK. We are content with each other and our Lord.

Later, we join Matt, Amy, Josh, Jennifer and the boys for a BBQ. I love my family so very much; God has used each of them to bless me beyond my greatest hopes.

*O**ur sons and daughters-in-law knew we all desperately needed to be together, especially as we navigated the challenges of my husband's health issues. We gathered for a BBQ at Matt and Amy's house in Salem. Lots of pictures were taken, followed by plenty of hugs, tears, and plans for the future.*

We finished the day with Dale officiating at the wedding of the son of some dear friends. Dale looked so handsome in his black suit that I purchased for him at Nordstrom's a few years ago. Dancing at the reception was a familiar and welcome bit of normal.

August 25, 2008

*I** was thankful we were surrounded by our children when Dr. Perosa told us that he did not even have to scope Dale's lung; the cancer had already eaten through the* *trachea and lymph nodes.*

We took Dale home and were quickly joined by many family members and friends. Despite the shock of recent events, Dale greeted everyone as graciously as ever. They responded to us with an outpouring of love, prayers and acts of kindness like we'd never experienced before. What a blessing to be held so closely by such dear people!

August 26, 2008

Dale's brother, Jim, and his wife, Peggy, drove up from California this morning, arriving in time for our 2 p.m. appointment with the pulmonary surgeon. The appointment where he would give us his final diagnosis of the cancer and the prognosis for Dale's treatment and recovery.

> *When something as scary as cancer hits close to home, you can't help thinking about yourself - your own age, health, and mortality. You start comparing your physical condition and health to that of others. But with Dale, there's not a lot of comparison going on because he is so alive, active, healthy, and energetic.*

> *What did we do after the initial shock wore off? Our family went into a fighting, researching and planning mode! We found out all we could about the best cancer-care facilities in the U.S., which ones offered the most comprehensive treatment programs and the doctors whose patients had the highest survival rates. To tell you the truth, researching cancer-treatment options was my main coping mechanism during this time! We hoped Dale's treatment could take place nearby, perhaps in Salem, Eugene, or even Portland. That*

way we could be close to them, and he and Ruby could be closer to their home, their church, and the camp. But the facilities and programs offered in those cities were just not at the same level as others a greater distance away.

They are at peace, conscious of God's perfect care and leading. He has so clearly opened some doors and closed others during this crucial time of gathering information so a choice can be made about the location, personnel, and medical procedures to pursue.

⊰⊱⊰⊱⊰

GOD EXPECTS me to live and to live fully unto Him. I'm a fighter, and with God and my family, I'm ready to tackle this opponent! My overall health is great (except for the cancer, obviously!), and my long history of outdoor activities has prepared me physically, emotionally, and physiologically for the aggressive treatments we'll pursue.

Ruby and Dale had such courage; they were convinced God would do a miracle of healing. It was hard for me to share their outlook because a family member of mine had terminal cancer and died. I couldn't stand the fact that Dale had to experience that amount of pain and fear.

From the very beginning of his ordeal, Dale refused to give in to the cancer diagnosis. He wouldn't give up and let cancer rule over his body. God and God alone would rule Dale Price, not fear or a medical condition.

⊸⥷⊸⥷

We all hoped for the best, of course, but in so many cancer cases, the person dies instead of getting healed. Those close to the Prices put their faith in God and prayed daily for his deliverance from cancer, but it was still hard to watch him suffer through the ordeal.

In the first month after the diagnosis, a special prayer time was organized for Dale. The elders met and prayed over him, following the instructions found in James 5. It's a testimony to the maturity of Dale's faith that he was sensitive to the possibility of sin in his life. He was very open with us, wanting us to really know him and ask questions that would help him make sure his life was in order. He didn't want sin or anything short of God's very best to hinder how the Lord might use him.

My time as a pastor and former missionary taught me that no one should do things alone. Especially tough things such as fighting cancer, like Dale was doing (even though he was used to doing stuff alone). Dale lived his cancer publicly, choosing to walk toward people in his journey with cancer. What a great example of transparency and community to people in and outside the church! He put on no mask, nor did he try to fool people about who he was and what was going on in his life.

⊸⥷⊸⥷

Many questions, few answers

As the family's research began to narrow down the viable options for Dale's treatment, much information was still needed before embarking on a course of action. Sometimes the volume of cancer data was simply overwhelming; occasionally the experts disagreed with one another; and hopes were sometimes dashed when a seemingly just-right treatment scenario didn't pan out.

Ruby and Dale's daughters-in-law, Amy and Jennifer, continued to do lots of research on the Internet. In addition to the hundreds of pages of information about lung cancer and its treatment they gathered, they helped set up several key medical consultations and appointments, and identified which doctors and hospitals were doing the best work with Dale's kind of cancer.

One conversation with a doctor during this time of intense research illustrated the difficulties Dale's family faced in finding excellent, available, and proven care:

> Us: "How many lung-cancer patients with a diagnosis similar to Dale's have you treated?"
>
> Doctor: "Three or four in the last four years."
>
> Us: "How are they doing now?"
>
> Doctor: "They're all dead."

Another discussion, also quite brief:

> Doctor: "Yes, I can definitely help him!"
>
> Us: "Great! How often have you supervised the kind of treatment program he'll need?"
>
> Doctor: "Well, that's the thing...I haven't yet. But I'm willing to give it a try."
>
> Us: "Um, thanks, but we'll keep looking."

A common response from the cancer professionals was,

"Because of the advanced nature of this cancer, we just can't do anything more for him." Fortunately, God had prepared the way for Dale to be treated at the Seattle Cancer Care Alliance (SCCA), a world-renowned partnership combining the cancer-treatment expertise, experience, and resources of the Fred Hutchinson Cancer Research Center, the University of Washington (UW) Medical Center, and Seattle Children's Hospital.

Dale and Ruby drove to Seattle to meet with SCCA's top oncologist (whose patients were still living!) to discuss strategies for quickly and aggressively battling the cancer. It was a very hope-instilling visit for the Prices, giving great encouragement to their family and anxious supporters.

The option of surgery on the tumor-riddled lung was discussed, too. Although attempting to clear out most or all of the cancer through an operation is often the best course of action, their lead surgeon, Dr. Wood, ruled it out. "At this advanced stage, taking out the diseased lung might actually encourage the cancer to spread and could even inhibit Dale's chances for recovery."

The proposed treatment plan would last approximately eight weeks, with regular doses of radiation and chemotherapy. Dale began the procedures, starting each of his days at the UW Medical Center. The concentrated radiation treatments were followed by intensive chemo for eight days. After eight days off the chemo, Dale was back on for eight more.

The Prices found God's caring hand present even in the mundane but serious matter of how they would pay for the super-expensive cancer treatments, hospital stays, medicines, lodging, meals, transportation, special assistance, and other expenses. But God knew what they'd need long before they did. Insurance benefits through Dale's former military service and family insurance covered the major part of this initial treatment.

Another advantage to receiving treatments in Seattle was their strong base of support from friends living in the Puget Sound region and the relatively close proximity of family members. Personal, appropriate and ongoing support was a critical component of the overall approach to successfully going through the treatment program. Support wasn't just for Dale and Ruby to receive either. Their sons, daughters in law, and grandsons needed Dale and Ruby's special love, too, to support them in their own struggles.

The CaringBridge connection

"This is the story of our journey with the Great Shepherd into the valley of the shadow of death. We have never felt closer to Him and to our friends and family. He is the Refiner and His fire does the work of making us more like Him. Praise God for His mercy and faithfulness. Love, Dale"

An online resource connecting people when a loved one is facing a significant health challenge, Dale and Ruby's personalized CaringBridge website kept thousands of people informed and encouraged during the cancer battle.

The Web tool, launched on September 1, 2008, allowed Dale and Ruby to share their hearts deeply and regularly with the friends and family who were eager to learn about and pray for the Prices.

Visitors to the site could read Dale's story, part of which is excerpted above, and journal, view photos, and contribute their own responses, encouragements, and prayers. Much more than simply a source of information about Dale's health, CaringBridge helped create a community of supporters worldwide.

The Prices' dear and longtime friend, Jaira Hill, took the lead in making sure CaringBridge friends received regular cancer-care updates, prayer requests, and personal messages from them:

"It's such a privilege to let others know how Dale is doing and convey his messages and teachings to the CaringBridge group. There's no way we can keep up with the hundreds of phone calls, cards, letters and emails, but the website lets us keep communicating with and supporting one another.

"In the very beginning, during some of the roughest days of treatment in Seattle, Dale and/or Ruby would dictate their thoughts and experiences, and I'd write up the messages and publish them on the site. Dale had important messages to share, words that would glorify the Lord and show how God was using the cancer journey to refine Dale and Ruby. He always wanted every message, even those that included some very discouraging news about his health, to have hope and to highlight the Bible verses God was using to strengthen Dale."

Fighting the good fight

About those early days, his colleagues and friends were watching carefully, looking for opportunities to come along the Price family.

> *From the beginning of his cancer journey, I thought Dale's outlook was Christlike and mature, and his expectations were realistic. His courage and determination were inspiring, and his hope contagious. I was one of the elders who anointed Dale with oil and prayed for his healing. All of us were humbled by the grace and goodness of God as we committed our brother, Dale, to His perfect care.*

> ༺༺༺

> *What stood out to me about how Dale handled his cancer was the way he kept a positive*

attitude, refusing to complain about his pain. He read and obeyed God's word with complete faith and trust, knowing that God's will for his life meant accepting a very difficult path.

And Ruby! She took such special care of Dale through this painful time, all the while keeping a positive outlook and holding to a firm faith.

I always had hope for his recovery, even when others gave up hope. I wasn't going to put limits on what God could do, despite the grim outlook and the fact that survival rates for this kind of cancer were extremely small.

"God expects me to live and to live fully unto Him. I'm a fighter, and with God and my family, I'm ready to tackle this opponent!"

STEP BY STEP

Victory comes, but it does so just one step at a time.

"AND THE LORD YOUR GOD WILL DRIVE OUT THOSE NATIONS BE-
FORE YOU LITTLE BY LITTLE; YOU WILL BE UNABLE TO DESTROY THEM
AT ONCE, LEST THE BEASTS OF THE FIELD BECOME TOO NUMEROUS
FOR YOU." DEUTERONOMY 7:22

Editor's note: *The following words are excerpted from the first entries on CaringBridge.*

September 9, 2008

Dale was rushed to a Salem hospital after starting to bleed from his hard coughing. The doctors were unable to stop the bleeding completely, even with the usually reliable cauterization.

It's good that the bleeding is gradual and not profuse. Please pray that it will stop - or at least not increase. Currently, his white- and red-blood counts are normal. If they stay the same until morning, he might be released so he can keep his appointment in Seattle with the cancer specialists (and begin chemo and radiation treatments). We are also concerned that the cancer has grown faster than expected, closing off Dale's right lung.

Daughter-in-law, Amy, just called from the hospital. She said that things are rough and they are all scared, but they know Dale will be held safe in God's hands, no matter what happens next.

Pray especially for Ruby. For awhile, she will be the only one with Dale in Seattle and will need all the support and strength that she can get.

They are at peace, being very conscious of God's care and leading through the entire process. He has opened some doors and closed others, guiding them through this crucial time of gathering informa-tion. Now they are confident of His leading as they make this hard decision regarding treatment.

September 12, 2008

Ruby called this afternoon with great news, saying, "God has made it clear we need to be in Seattle for treatment. We met with Dr. Martins who told us, 'We can treat this.' Prior to our appointment he studied all of Dale's x-rays, MRIs, etc., and said that Dale's cancer is absolutely treatable."

Dr. Martins is the No. 1 lung-, throat- and head-cancer special-ist at the Fred Hutchinson Clinic in Seattle. Dale's team includes Dr. Martins; Dr. Woods, a surgeon; and Dr. Patel, a radiation oncologist. Ruby said the team has the newest and best technology and knowl-edge at their fingertips.

Dale and Ruby will be home this weekend to pack up and move to an apartment in Seattle; radiation treatment begins Thursday, with chemotherapy scheduled to begin on September 22. The planned treatment runs for eight weeks and Dale and Ruby are expecting to stay in Seattle for the duration.

The Prices have been praying for clear direction regarding the doctors and other medical providers who would initiate and guide the grueling treatment process. They felt God's hand on their meet-ing with Dr. Martins and Dr. Patel. As Dale put it, "God put together this entire cancer-care team. Everyone at SCCA is wonderful, treating us like we were the only people they planned to see the rest of the day!"

September 13, 2008

Dale and Ruby asked that we pray specifically for these needs:

1) Housing. They need to find an apartment for their eight-week stay in Seattle. Ruby wants a place where she can cook for Dale. He is determined to keep up his strength because, as the radiologist explained, he will be able to receive stronger doses of the treatment if he is able to eat healthily and exercise regularly.

2) Migraines. Dale has had debilitating migraines this week.

3) Nausea. Dale really needs to eat so his weight stays stable, but eating is difficult, if not impossible, with constant waves of nausea washing over him.

4) The start of radiation treatments on Thursday.

5) The start of chemotherapy on Monday.

6) Friday's meeting with Dr. Woods, the nation's foremost thoracic surgeon.

Dale and Ruby have been blessed by the many cards they have re-ceived, and by the messages many of you have left on the CaringBridge website. God bless you.

Moon Rise

by Elaine Roemen

Chapter 2

Starting Strong

"By God's grace I will run the race God has set before me, running with the hope and courage you, my family and brothers and sisters, have come to count on. I will be a better man, husband, father, grandfather and friend because you have helped me put on God's armor and cheered me on as I have followed my Savior into the battle."

Knowing something about a person's background helps us better understand who they are today and how they got that way. For those who first met Dale and Ruby at Canyonview Camp, Silverton First Baptist, or during Ruby's days as an educator, the story of their youth and beyond is a fascinating account of God's grace, strong families, and their unquenchable desire to live life to the brim.

Beginnings

The second oldest of five, Ruby Price grew up in a Christian home where "everything we did revolved around God. We always knew that God came first, God's work came second and everything else came third."

Ruby's father, Dr. Ernest Campbell, had the initial vision for Canyonview Camp. The camp's beautiful 80-acre location straddles Drift Creek, east of Salem, Ore., between Silverton and Sublimity. The ministry's goal is still as powerful as it was then: Help young people know the Bible, find Christ and have fun outdoors.

The family moved there when Ruby was in the seventh grade, and she and her sisters attended the little school just down the road. For high school, she went to a private Christian school in Salem. Ruby received a bit of a discount on her tuition because her mother Fern drove several Silverton-area children back and forth.

Ruby had to earn her own money for school clothes, which she did by selling the eggs from the family's chickens and by picking berries.

In addition to her church and school activities, Ruby was an avid reader. She found and devoured books from many authors, covering many fields of interest. Reading helped set the stage for her successful career as a teacher, principal, superintendent, education consultant, trainer, speaker, curriculum developer.

Ruby was outgoing and always on the lookout for someone who might need a friend. Years later, one of them remembered the time when 13-year-old Ruby took an interest in a shy 7-year-old girl from a "very messed-up family."

> *We were in the same neighborhood as the Campbells and one day Ruby asked if I wanted to go to church with her. I couldn't believe it. Not only that a cool teenager invited me to do something with her, but that my folks let me go!*

From their family's earliest days, Nelson and Barbara Price kept first things first. Both parents were educators, but it was their love for God and family that made Dale's growing-up years so rich, helping direct his choices for the rest of his life.

Dale's dad influenced him in innumerable ways, ways that would show up particularly in Dale's approach to Christian camping. Nelson Price was always busy and productive, adding on to the family home; building a new patio; researching and writing genealogy; or organizing pictures for the family album.

The family was very close, not only as Dale and his siblings grew up, but throughout the years that followed. Vacations, reunions, birthdays, holidays – the Prices never missed an opportunity to get together. Jim Price says, "Dale and I were buddies from the very beginning, doing everything together. We watched 'Gunsmoke,' ate popcorn with our parents, and played football and baseball. We even found creative ways to torment our little brother, Bill, and sister, Ellen!"

The family always had room for others, too.

> *I knew I was always welcome in their home, and it was comforting to be included in such a*

stable and loving family. It has made all of the difference in my life.

I was so impressed with the family and how at home I felt with each one of them. My heart was deeply touched, and I felt as if I had been with them forever! Right from the start they made me feel so at ease; I felt like I was a member of the Price Bunch!

We were always joking and having a ball together. I couldn't get over the great dynamics in the family. I thought it then and still do now: I love this family and I feel so blessed to be a part of it.

In the beginning Dale teased me, but also took time to talk with me in depth. Eventually, he really took me under his wing as he became a true mentor to me. We were just like brother and sister, and he would always ask me, "How are you really doing?"

During his years growing up in Glendora, Calif., Dale was active in the Boy Scouts and developed a great love for hiking and exploring God's creation. A childhood friend remembers those days fondly and vividly:

"We met in 1958, when we were 11 years old. Dale and I were assigned to the Panther Patrol and became not only assistant patrol leaders, but also best friends. Our time in Boy Scouts was very important to both of us and we continued with Troop 486 all the way through high school, both of us attaining the rank of Eagle Scout.

"We camped, hiked and cooked outdoors throughout our teenage years, and at the age of 16, became counselors at Camp Cherry Valley, a Boy Scout summer camp located near a beautiful beach on Santa Catalina Island. This was a highlight of our teenage years, spending two summers teaching camping, pioneering, handicrafts, cooking and other skills.

"We lived in 8' x 8' open-air cabins, complete with washrooms without walls and cold showers. The camp lacked a cabin when we arrived the first year and, as his father undoubtedly would have done, Dale quickly built a new one. That cabin became Dale's home for those two summers. And, it was good preparation for Dale's future vocation and ministry. Years later he would build most of an entire camp called Canyonview.

"We also worked on the waterfront, teaching swimming, lifesaving, canoeing and rowing. The water was crystal clear and fairly warm, complete with flying fish, orange garibaldi, and porpoises.

"We would sleep out under the stars when we could, often climbing about 500 yards above the Price home into the Southern California brush, rolling out our sleeping bags, and falling asleep as we looked out at the shimmering lights of Los Angeles.

"Once we got our drivers licenses, we put them to immediate (and frequent) use, usually jumping into his '57 Dodge or my '58 Chevy, and heading out to the beach to body surf and soak up the sun. The beaches weren't our only destination. no sir! From time to time we would get a hankering for a date milkshake and drive out to Thousand Palms or some other suitable desert locale. A two- or three-hour drive into the desert, just for a milkshake? Hey, Dale and I were young, had wheels and, seemingly, all the time in the world!

"Those were great years. When it came to trying new endeavors – and he almost always succeeded at them – no one lived life like Dale Price. One time he decided he liked the guitar and thought he should learn to play it. Even though he had no prior musical experience, his attitude was, No problem, I'll just figure it out. He picked one up and started teaching himself to play. It wouldn't be too many years after that before Dale, aka Buzzard, was leading songs at Canyonview campfires, guitar slung over his shoulder, with a big, welcoming smile on his face.

"After our senior year in high school, he signed up for a summer-long youth bicycle tour through Europe. To the Canyonview campers and staff members who followed Dale on bike trips throughout Oregon, Washington, and Canada for days, if not weeks, knowing this bit of history might produce a knowing smile. "So that's where Buzzard got the idea for these long-distance bicycle adventures!"

College days

After high school, Dale applied to and was accepted at Oregon State University. Dale received a Reserved Officers' Training Corps (ROTC) scholarship while at the university, helping launch his career as an officer in the U.S. Army.

The day came to leave home and family and make the 24-hour bus ride from Southern California to the center of the Willamette Valley in Oregon. Dressed in what was then the standard-issue uniform for boys in L.A. – white t-shirt, Levis, white socks, blue dockside shoes, and poplin jacket – Dale began a brand-new adventure, one that would change not only his life, but, ultimately, the lives of thousands.

Once he was in Oregon, Dale fell in love with the state's rugged beauty, endless opportunities for recreation, and the crisp, clear autumn air that greeted him when he arrived in Corvallis. In fact, his initial experiences and impressions were so deep and lasting, he became a lifelong Oregonian.

Dale and Chuck were roommates at OSU, continuing their re-lationship and making more friends at their dorm, Weatherford Hall. They had great times ("Probably not so great for our grades, though," Chuck recalled) on campus, including long and passionate discussions with other students about philosophy, Vietnam, science, and religion.

It was during Dale's junior year, after he'd moved off campus to the Sigma Nu fraternity house, that he first met a beautiful Christian girl, Ruby Campbell. After discovering they had strong feelings for one another, they began dating one another exclusively. Eventually, they even talked about the very real possibility that God meant for them to be together for much longer - and for much more - than just their college years.

But when Dale graduated the following year, they realized that the Army's plans for Dale's future were quite different from theirs. 2nd Lieutenant Dale Price was being sent to Germany to begin a four-year tour of duty. While he wouldn't have to face the dangers of war in Vietnam, the love of his life would be more than 5,000 miles away. Dale asked Ruby five times to marry him. At first, she didn't think he was serious. Then she thought she was too young. Well, then, she wasn't sure.

In 1969, Dale and Ruby had to give God their fears about the future, trusting Him with their relationship. They didn't know what it might become and whether they would be together or apart. It was a time of learning to place their faith in the only

"I don't pretend to understand all that God is doing through us while on this journey, but He is working. Step by step. Walking the way of the good Shepherd makes me ask: If we are not ready to trust Him with our present and its circumstances – which lasts but a brief time – how can we begin to trust Him with our eternity?"

One who could see their path and guide their steps. The lessons in faith they learned as young people laid the foundation for the even-greater faith they would need later in life.

Just before Dale boarded his army transport to Germany, he called Ruby to ask her one last time if she would accept his proposal of marriage. With seconds before he had to board the plane, she replied, "Yes." Dale still had to get on that army transport to Germany, but within 2 1/2 weeks of his arrival in Germany, he asked his commanding officer for leave to return to Oregon to get married. The response was, "Lieutenant, why didn't you take care of that before you got here?"

Leave was granted, and Dale returned to Oregon so he could marry his sweetheart. Ten days after the wedding, Dale returned to Germany with his new bride, where they stayed so he could complete his active-duty assignment with the Army.

After serving in Germany for four years, Dale decided to resign from active duty. He continued his career in the Army Reserves up until 1999, at which point he had achieved the rank of Colonel.

Ministry at Canyonview and beyond

Four years after getting married, Dale and Ruby received the call from her parents to come back to Oregon, specifically to Canyonview, to begin the camping program ministry on the grounds where Ruby grew up. They joined forces with Ruby's family to turn the dreams of a year-round camp for all ages into reality. Much more than a kid's camp, Canyonview came to encompass multiple overnight, weekend and day camps; Bible Teaching, Inc.; a seminary; a printing and publication shop; and an equestrian center/college.

Dale and Ruby focused their lives on loving people and spreading the Gospel to every person who came on the Canyonview grounds. Dale's love for the outdoors also resulted in a brand-new ministry away from the Canyonview Camp property. Every year, hundreds of youth and adults participated in backpacking, bicycle, sailing, and wilderness adventures, usually led by Dale and always designed to implant God's word, develop young Christian leaders, and provide an unsurpassed experience in God's magnificent creation.

When we left military life and moved back to Oregon, Dale and I were ready to create something new. Not only in terms of a camping ministry, but in how we as a couple would live out our marriage, interact with others, and conduct our individual ministries.

I was ready to return to the camp and many of the people I'd known as a girl, but I didn't want to just fall into the old patterns and activities from those growing-up years. Frankly, Dale and I weren't like a lot of Christian leaders we knew, but because we were very strong in our relationship and our trust in God's direction in our lives, we could do things differently and know we'd remain close.

We served together at Canyonview for 10 years (until I began my career in education), sharing in all aspects of the ministry and work. It wasn't just Dale doing it all and me staying at home. During that decade I led or co-led nearly everything: adventure camps (hiking, biking, sailing, wilderness camping and backpacking); the day-camp program; and women's ministries.

Ruby's teaching, leadership and mentoring roles at Canyonview allowed her to build lifelong relationships with many women. There was a special affinity between Ruby and several stay-at-home moms, deepening friendships that continue today.

Dale was busy outside of camp, too, meeting regularly with

other pastors in the community; preaching and teaching in numerous churches, conferences and schools; leading prayer meetings; and participating in other ministry opportunities.

Dale had been the interim pastor of Silverton First Baptist Church for about sixteen months when I was called as pastor in 1989. For the next 22 years, our relationship grew. We respected and truly loved one another as we served the Lord and His people in the church, and in other ministry opportunities.

In 2004, Dale and I joined our church's newly formed council of elders, giving us a chance to form an even deeper bond. I'm so glad Dale remained in the same fellowship where he had been interim pastor, because his example showed me how men of God – whether their role was as the current, interim or former pastor – could serve effectively together.

When I met Dale I met much more than church's interim pastor. His presence in the community was huge. In a way, Dale Price embodied parachurch ministry in our area because he was doing it to a greater degree and with greater effect than almost anyone. We connected personally and spiritually during our elder meetings, and discovered our similarities. And differences!

Dale's creativity, initiative, leadership and dreams were painted everywhere on the canvas called Canyonview Camp. The more I learned about the camp, the more I asked, Why isn't our church harnessing the skill, passion, and vision of its members, like what Dale has done at Canyonview? How can our church accomplish as much done as Dale and his team does at the camp?

Campers and staff: We were there and we remember

In 1981 I came to Canyonview to attend the seminary where Dale was an instructor. In time, I was hired and began helping with projects around the camp. Whether it was serving meals, fixing whatever was broken, or starting construction on a new building, Dale and I worked shoulder to shoulder for years.

I think our work habits complemented one another and helped us get a lot done. I loved the fact that Dale never complained, never avoided tough jobs, or said, "This is impossible. We can't do this."

We quickly found that our attitudes about what could be accomplished in the lives of young people through Christian camping was similar, too. The wilderness trips, in particular, provided great opportunities for people to grow personally and share the Lord in beautiful outdoor settings.

When he got cancer it was hard for all of us. Very, very hard. He'd been the only leader we'd had, whether you'd been on staff for 30 days or 30 years. The questions came quickly and mostly without answers. Where would we find what only he could bring to this ministry? How are we going to follow effectively in the path he's set before us?

Dale left an imprint, not of Dale Price and his accomplishments, but of God's work and Word.

༺ ༻

Our family was deeply involved at Canyonview for many years, years that saw incredible growth in the camp's ministry. Hundreds, maybe thousands of people, had their lives changed forever when they met Christ for the first time while at the camp.

We took on plenty of construction projects around the grounds, and several of the buildings were designed by Dale. It was hard work, sure, but through it all there was lots of laughter and fun. Those first families – Dale and Ruby's, ours and others - put a lot of themselves into Canyonview. We were active and close,and were always challenging one another in our games and contests.

One of Dale's signature programs was Teens in Ministry (TIM). In it, high school and college students were trained in all aspects of the Christian camping ministry, from wilderness skills, to counseling, to horsemanship, and water sports. Scores of young women and men were changed by the TIM program, led by Dale and Ruby. Many of the TIM participants had been campers who found Christ, friends and more at camp.

The main reason Canyonview's ministry has been so effective for so long is that Dale wanted the camp to be a safe haven. Safe for everyone, but especially for those young people who came from broken homes, abusive relationships, and other difficult situations. The camp gave them a chance to learn, grow and change. Most of all, the camp's programs gave kids and young adults the Gospel message and the opportunity to invite Jesus Christ into their lives.

⊰⊱⊰

I believe I was about 1975 when my sister saw an ad in the newspaper for a horse camp near our home in Salem, Ore. She begged our mom to let her go and, thankfully, Mom said yes. As a result of my sister going to Canyonview, our entire family was changed. Forever.

My mom, my sister and my brother all came to know Jesus as Savior because they found authentic people at Canyonview, and heard a biblical message that was exactly what they needed. They saw, especially in the lives of Dale and Ruby Price, what it meant to live a life dedicated to Jesus Christ, focused on nurturing healthy relationships with people.

in the Canyonview staff, my sister found a family; in Dale, my brother found a father; and in Ruby's dad, Ernie Campbell, my mom found a mentor.

No, I wasn't on that list of family members who were blessed by the ministries of Canyonview Camp because at that time I was busy feeding my bitterness and anger about my broken home. I ran away at 16 and devoted myself to rebellion and drugs. It took me years to come to God, but when I was ready, Dale and Ruby were there. Even when I had given up on myself, they hadn't. They never stopped loving me; they never quit believing in me.

◆◆◆

I loved learning God's Word from Dale, especially when us kids pedaled our bikes up and down those hills in the San Juan Islands and on Vancouver Island with him and Ruby. I also loved babysitting the Prices' boys and seeing their marriage in action, a marriage that reflected God's love so beautifully.

◆◆◆

"When we abide, we find His peace. Abiding in Him means abiding in His joy. Abiding in Him means we can see the beauty of the Savior, regardless of circumstances.

"When we abide, we realize there is nothing that can separate us from the love of Christ Jesus."

I was always blessed by Dale's leadership, teaching, insights, and who he was as a person. When I was a first-time camper he told me that if the only reason I was at camp was for the horses, then I was in the wrong place. It's not about the horses, Dale said, it's about God. I didn't understand at first, but when I did it completely changed my experience at Canyonview.

∽⁖∽⁖∽⁖

Canyonview's ministry continued to grow as it reached more children and families for Christ. The organization, as well, expanded and improved. A new internship program, a more fully developed Equestrian College, additional camping ministries, completion of facility improvements, and a reorganized and better-trained staff are evidence of God's ongoing care and blessing.

Superintendent Price

*T*oday I began work as superintendent of a small school district on the southern Oregon coast, about four and a half hours away from our home in Silverton.

When I applied for and was being considered for the

position, Dale and I knew the distance and logistics would be challenging, but we also knew the job represented an in-credible opportunity to re-enter my profession, educational leadership.

There would be, of course, times of separation and Dale would need to adjust his schedule. But there would also be wonderful times of togetherness in a new place. As it turned out, we walked more beaches, hiked and biked more trails, and ate out in more special restaurants than we had for years. Although balancing the care needs of our dads proved to be more difficult than we had anticipated, our life was together was good and we were so blessed.

⚘⚘⚘

I met Ruby when we were conducting a search for Port Orford/Langlois school district's next superintendent. Ruby had not been a school superintendent before, but we really liked her energy, her teaching and leadership background, and her willingness to think outside the box.

Our committee found many things to like about Ruby, more than enough to qualify her for the position, but one example of the quality of her character and experience was particularly striking.

When she arrived at a former school as the principal, there was graffiti on the walls of the school, children were not attending, the staff was discouraged, and there were many other problems. She and her team (including people from the community) started removing all the graffiti from the walls. This completely changed the school's outer appearance, but the greatest changes occurred inside. Under Ruby's leadership attendance greatly improved, test *scores went up and the faculty and staff were fully engaged with the students and their families.*

Of course, we hired Ruby as our superintendent and hit the ground running! A few months after the start of our school year, we did some remodeling at the high school. I got to work with her husband, Dale, building some cabinets and moving furniture. As anyone who has worked alongside Dale Price can tell you, his energy and stick-to-it attitude are second to none. He could easily work me into the ground!

After I spent some time around Ruby and Dale, I was struck with how happy they were, just being together. Individually and as a couple, they had a powerful influence on others. Once you met them you wanted to spend as much time with them as you could.

Joe Brown, former chair, Port Orford/Langlois School District

To Russia, with the love of Christ

Deapte her demanding work as a superintendent, Ruby never missed a doctor's appointment with Dale. But Dale wsn't sitting around doing nothing while she worked; he continue to work, too. The camp always was in need of his help, guidance and direction, and then, he received a phone call, inviting him to Russia to speak in January 2009. Dale wrote on CaringBridge:

I HAVE been asked by the president of Christian Camping Russia and by Global Outreach, the worldwide outreach of the Christian Camp and Conference Association (CCCA), to be the keynote speaker at the former Soviet

Union's national Christian-camping conference. Please
pray that my visa and all the travel arrangements will come
together. But, most of all, pray that I will be able to bring
messages of hope and encouragement to these amazing
Russian Christian leaders. I'll keep you posted as we see
God's perfect will unfolding....

January 29, 2009

I ARRIVED safe and sound in St. Petersburg, knowing
God has prepared a great time of ministry and challenge for
me and those attending.

The skies are semi-cloudy and the temperature hovers
between 10 and 15 degrees. Walking distances between
buildings are short, so the cold doesn't penetrate our cloth-
ing - except on the day we decided to play in the snow. I
couldn't resist the fun of creating a snowman in Russia with
three creative, young camp leaders.

The conference, held at a former Soviet facility near
the frozen Gulf of Finland, brought together about 230
Christian camping leaders from as far away as Vladivostok,
Siberia, the Ukraine, Latvia, Estonia, and even Israel. Most
had traveled at their own expense, took unpaid time away
from work, and covered their own conference costs. It was
very humbling to know that God had given me a key part of
what they were going to gain from the conference.

Those attending were mostly 18 to 35 years old, men
and women, filled with a zeal to learn and then return to
more effectively minister. Many had been leading camps
since they were in their teens.

The warmth of fellowship was irresistible at mealtimes,
at the seminars and during the evening worship and teaching times. It is amazing how quickly strangers who share a
common faith and a common love for seeing young people

find Christ, can become brothers and sisters.

The conference was took place at a facility that had been used by the Communists for one of their Young Pioneer camps. The Soviets used these camps to build strong allegiance to the Communist system as well engage in healthy, team-building activities.

At the meetings over the next few days I will be teaching from the first five chapters of 2 Corinthians. God knew all along He'd want to use me here in Russia; that is why my life has been preserved, despite the cancer I carry with me. In my speaking I know I sometimes fumbled, missed key points and got too theological, but God used my efforts through the empowering work of the Holy Spirit.

I shared most of the epistle to the Philippians during the keynote presentations and wrote out Bible-study questions for people to explore each morning in small groups. Then, in the evenings, I taught from the same passage they had studied that morning. I also taught two workshops for smaller groups, "Developing Spiritual Strength" and "Evaluating the Effectiveness of Your Camping Ministry."

In all of this teaching and sharing, I was blessed with wonderful translators. Nikolai translated my keynote addresses and Marina translated my daily conversations with people, as well as the six hours of seminars and about 10 additional hours of biblical counseling with individuals. These sisters in Christ helped me build many wonderful friendships through their gift of translation.

I led three two-hour seminars on topics of concern to anyone involved in the camp ministry: depression, burnout and discouragement. Those sessions resulted in individual counseling opportunities that lasted two to three hours each day. It was clear that this also was a key part of God's plan for my trip. Since many of the counselees were women, Marina's presence was invaluable.

Days and evenings at the conference flew by. It was non-stop studying, fellowshipping, eating, singing, teaching, and praying. I am journaling the events of the week and the many answers to prayer, and will share these soon.

One day I went for a walk and found my way to the Gulf of Finland. The water was frozen for as far as I could see and the sun was shining. As I walked and recorded my journey on my digital camera, I decided I needed a picture of myself. I saw two women walking on the ice and asked them to take my picture. They answered, in perfect English, "Yes, of course."

We walked and talked and they invited me in for tea at the summer house (dacha) they were renting for the week-end. Over the course of several hours I was able to share with them the story of my cancer, of God's love, and His kindness toward Ruby and I through Christ. Thankfully, they were full of questions and a bond of friendship was forged.

When I returned to the camp and told my translators about the encounter, they said, "This never happens." The women's openness and willingness to talk about spiritual things - not to mention the fact that they spoke English - was all miraculous. I believe it was truly a divine appointment, an opening sent by God allowing me to share His truth and love with two souls who really needed to hear the Good News.

Let me share one more brief, but amazing, answer to prayer. During the six keynote sessions I coughed only once. That one time was when I was describing our cancer adventures. Considering that I was coughing almost nonstop for weeks before the conference, it was clearly the hand of God calming my lung in order to get His message out.

February 17, 2009

I have been home from St. Petersburg, Russia, for a little over a week now. To say the trip and the ministry were fantastic would be an understatement! I'm grateful to the Northwest Section of the Christian Camp and Conference Association, which helped fund my trip, and to Canyonview, for allowing me to go while others handled my camp responsibilities.

STEP BY STEP

Editor's note: *The Step by Step entries throughout the rest of the book are taken from Dale and Ruby's CaringBridge messages to friends and family.*

September 18, 2008

Dale began the first of his radiation treatments today at the University of Washington. It involves high-dosage, intensive therapy, much stronger than anything he could have received in Salem. "Hey, "I'm glowing in the dark!" he says. "Literally!" I'm thankful that God has given me the opportunity to share my faith with medical personnel and other patients every day."

Dale and Ruby are grateful for everyone's prayers. God opened a previously closed door so they can now move into the Pete Gross House (a special residence for cancer patients), providing them with a wonderful home away from home while they're in Seattle for Dale's initial treatments.

The apartment is just three blocks from the treatment center and one mile from downtown, so Dale and Ruby will have plenty of opportunities for walking. "We are so very blessed by our living situation!" Among the amenities is a rooftop patio offering beautiful views of the Space Needle, Lake Union and the Olympic Mountains.

September 21, 2008

Dale has completed the second of his 31 radiation treatments. The other cancer treatments, chemotherapy, begin on Monday and continue for 10 days.

The doctors told Dale he must keep up his strength up, so he can receive the maximum possible dosage during the treatments. So, Dale and Ruby joined 24-Hour Fitness (receiving a special rate for cancer patients!). The regular exercise not only helps Dale maintain his strength and flexibility, it gives them — especially Ruby — a much-needed change of scenery.

Knowing that people are praying blesses and encourages Dale and Ruby as they embark on the demanding course set before them. Ruby estimates there are more than 2000 people praying for Dale. Besides family members and friends across America and beyond, entire churches around the world are dedicated to praying for the Prices. Incredible!

September 25, 2008

As I receive my second dose of chemo, I am sobered by the realization that I am on a path that's pretty steep. I don't pretend to understand all that God is doing through us while we're on this journey, but He is working. Step by step. Walking the way of the good Shepherd makes me ask: If we are not ready to trust Him with our present and its circumstances – which lasts but a brief time – how can we begin to trust Him with our eternity?

September 26, 2008

Last night was Date Night! Ruby and I had great seats for the Neil Diamond concert, just four rows from the stage! I got some extra sleep and was able to reschedule my radiation treatment so I'd be rested and ready for a wonderful evening of music with my beautiful bride.

The chemotherapy is not as bad as they were expecting. As the doctors infuse Dale with the treatment, they are also infusing him with powerful anti-nausea medicine. The nausea lingers, Dale says, but he hasn't thrown up, and he is eating. The nausea is supposed to ease up about three days after he stops the chemo, so by about Thursday of next week, Dale should be getting relief from the nausea.

What's next? This round of chemo ends Monday and then there's a 21-day reprieve until the next six-day round begins. Meanwhile, radiation continues every day, Monday through Friday, for another five weeks.

Dale shared his faith with a nurse named Mary, urging her to consider a relationship with God based on abiding in His love, instead of being caught up in religion. She acknowledged that Dale's faith seemed to work for him, but didn't appear to be interested in accepting the Lord and His salvation. Remember to pray for Mary.

September 28, 2008

Dale and Ruby had a very busy, very rewarding weekend. Their son, daughter-in-law and grandsons visited, as well as Dale's sister, Ellen (all the way from Fresno). Then Drew and Stacy, friends from Canyonview Camp, also stopped by briefly to videotape Dale's message for the camp's big auction on Nov. 1. The Prices are looking ahead to Tuesday when Dale's 90-year-

old father, Nelson, and Dale's sister-in-law, Peggy, will stop by.

October 2, 2008

Dale had an MRI in order to try to find the cause of his severe headaches. We are praising God because not only did the doctor tell Dale his brain appeared to be "perfect" (she said it looked like the brain of a 25-year-old!), the headaches are gone!

We continue to draw closer to the Lord, especially in the days since moving to Seattle. Here are some of the assurances the Lord has been giving us:

You can't abide in what's past or yet to come - God calls us to abide with Him in the here-and-now.

When we abide, we find His peace.

Abiding in Him means abiding in His joy.

Abiding in Him means we can see the beauty of the Savior, regardless of circumstances.

When we abide, we realize there is nothing that can separate us from the love of Christ Jesus.

We are His own precious possession, safe forever in the palm of His hand.

October 14, 2008

We continue to be blessed - by cards and CaringBridge messages; prayers for healing; faithful friends; good insurance coverage; the Pete Gross House; this beautiful and interesting city; my overall health; time together; the Canyonview team that is filling in all the gaps; and so much more.

"My prayer remains the same, as it has been from the first day I was diagnosed, that Christ would be exalted either by my death or by my life. My task is to keep on walking through this valley of death with Him. I know He is the one leading and the One holding my hand."

The doctor said I'm doing fantastic. Today marks my 19th day of radiation, with 18 more to go. The other part of my treatment plan, chemotherapy, starts next Monday and goes for a week (but I get the weekend off). The doctor said I shouldn't expect to feel as good as I do now, but I want to prove him wrong!

November 3, 2008

Lord willing, we leave Seattle for home in five days, on November 7! The goal while there is to get stronger, in order to better fight the cancer and to allow the treatments to have their maximum benefit. According to the doctors, the effects of the chemo will continue in my body for several weeks and the radiation will continue to have an effect for several months.

Periodic blood work will be done in Silverton and sent to Seattle for analysis. Then, next month, we return to Seattle for a CAT scan, blood work and several doctors' appointments. We are praying that the CAT scan will show that the treatments have had their desired effects.

November 4, 2008

As the nurse is dressing my wounds and prepping me to receive an injection, she asks, "How can you and Ruby be so happy?" After telling her how and why God has blessed us and our relationship, I ask her if there is anything I can pray about for her.

"My husband and I have been trying to get pregnant for 13 years, but so far we've been unsuccessful." So, Ruby and I prayed with her, right there in the middle of the busy hospital, with its sophisticated medical equipment and highly trained personnel.

Two months later, she caught up with us and exclaimed, "I'm expecting!!" What an opportunity for God to be glorified and a family to know about the power of prayer.

Early each morning, before starting the chemo treatments at the U of W, I'd usually wake up to a special time when God and I could talk.

Placing my hand on the place where the cancer was, I'd call out, "God, You know me, You know my name and I know that You love me. You know every cell in my body, the ones that are healthy and those that are trying to destroy the healthy ones." Then, I'd be at peace. His strengthening hand and comforting presence in the room keeps me from despair and worry.

November 9, 2008

We're home! Praise God! After some very challenging packing maneuvers (how did we accumulate all these things in just eight weeks?) we got on the road, eventually pulling into our driveway in Silverton about 8:30 p.m.

What a blessed sight greeted us as we entered our home! The deaconesses from Silverton First Baptist had cleaned our house top to bottom. Windows cleaned; kitchen curtains washed and pressed; shelves dusted; and carpets vacuumed. Two dear friends built us a little pump house. The freezer we hadn't the time or energy to move up from the camp had been moved into our basement (food and all!) by some dear brothers and sisters. They had even gotten rid of our old freezer.

How does it feel to be home? Well, it feels wonderful to be here, so much closer to family and friends. But, at the same time, it seems a little strange to be away from the city where we were so blessed, the place where God was increasingly giving us spheres of ministry. We'll miss Seattle, but go back in December for some crucial tests, and every three months after that.

Our prayer, as we re-enter our familiar world, is that we live life with the same spiritual intensity that has characterized our lives since I was first diagnosed. As I work to get stronger, undergo blood tests and await the diagnosis in December, we must continue abiding in Christ.

My prayer remains the same, as it has been from the first day I was diagnosed, that Christ would be exalted either by my death or by my life. My task is to keep on walking through this valley of death with Him. I know He is the one leading and the One holding my hand. That is my strength and comfort.

December 16, 2008

For the past month we have focused on strengthening my health, our marriage and our family.

We returned to Seattle yesterday so I could meet with my neurologist. I was happy to tell her that I had been off all medications for more than a month, with no headaches. I had blood drawn for the lab analysis and had a CAT scan.

Tomorrow we will meet with my doctors and find out how my body (and the cancer) has responded to the radiation and chemotherapy treatments we began nearly three months ago.

Chapter 3

This Has Not Taken God by Surprise

"There is comfort in knowing God is not caught off guard, even if we are. He continues to be the source of our hope and comfort. We didn't choose this path, but every day we choose Him who made this path and walks with us each step of the way.

"Our choice is clear: Trust God and walk with Him in the light of His perfect plan, or trust in something less. And stumble in the darkness."

Choosing God's way

From childhood on, Dale and Ruby Price understood that God's purposes in their lives were not only for His glory, those purposes were for their own good. Their growth. Their ability to serve others. Their preparation for the road ahead

Very early in his cancer journey, Dale believed that God intended to use the unwanted and destructive disease for the greatest ministry opportunity of his life. The cancer part of God's plan, set in place long before Dale was born, allowed thousands around the world to see what trusting fully in God really meant.

As time went on and as the cancer progressed, Dale and Ruby were changed and refined. They never doubted the decision to trust the Great Physician. The reality of their God-honoring choices meant that some people didn't understand – or, in some cases, didn't approve of – their decisions. Why didn't they just surrender to the so-called "inevitable," move to Hawaii, and live out Dale's remaining days pursuing as much relaxation and pain reduction as they could?

For the Prices, the questions about how long Dale had and what would happen next were answered by nothing more (or nothing less!) than their Lord's promises: "My grace is sufficient for you... I will never leave you nor forsake you... God is the strength of my heart and my portion forever."

Some people may have thought that Dale and Ruby's faith and choice to walk with God somehow spared them from fears, questions, and uncertainties about their future.

Not true.

Questions and answers

Fear, discouragement, even anger were never far from them, but the difference was in how they chose to live. They consciously, purposely chose a high-definition life. That kind of life meant they lived with their eyes wide open, intent on realizing the prize of Christ's high calling on their lives. Simultaneously, other, lesser pursuits and pleasures faded from view.

Of all the questions Dale asked God, one was particularly important, both because of how frequently it was asked and the life-changing results of its answer: "God, what are You trying to do in and through me **right now**?"

The answer to that question, asked daily (if not hourly), gave Dale and Ruby their marching orders. And, as they walked according to the Lord's instruction, the Prices found the greatest satisfaction any child of God can hope for: Knowing they were living obediently, joyfully, in His moment-by-moment purposes and provisions. Furthermore, God was reaping a great harvest of faith in the lives of the thousands worldwide who witnessed Dale's cancer journey.

"THEREFORE, SINCE WE HAVE SO GREAT A CLOUD OF WITNESSES SURROUNDING US, LET US...RUN WITH ENDURANCE THE RACE THAT IS SET BEFORE US." HEBREWS 12:1

Dale and Ruby chose to trust God for each step along their path, without knowing what the next rise, bend or narrow

Dale had confidence that God was still working for his good, even though the cancer was not a good thing. He didn't know if he would beat it or not, but he was going to do all he could to fight it. And, during the fight, Dale was determined to continue serving Christ and people, in whatever way he could.

passageway would bring – let alone when and how the journey would conclude.

Unanswered questions – especially the Why? questions – were part of the experience, too. The questions came on the five-hour drives to Seattle for radiation treatments. In hospital waiting rooms. Staring at the ceiling in the dark, when sleep would not come.

Why?

AND, OVER time, the Why questions were replaced by How questions. From "Why did this happen?" and "Why does it seem like every victory in the fight against cancer is followed by a setback" to "How can I be God's man right here, right now?" and "How can I keep my eyes fixed on my Savior, when circumstances constantly cloud and distract my view?" "How will my family see Christ in me today?"

Dale and I had to acknowledge and work through the loss of our dreams for our future. No longer counting on the possibilities that retirement and new ministry opportunities would bring. Not being able to build a house of our own, after years of living in those of others. No planning for the years ahead that would finally, wonderfully, be ours.

We had to let it all go. Leave those things in God's hands. Seek the Who – our Savior – not the Why.

Part of the roller-coaster ride is not knowing if the next chemo treatment or new drug is going to work. You begin to plan, to hope, but there are no guarantees. We live in the moment, from appointment to appointment, from test result to test result, not making plans beyond the present.

God and His sufficiency became the one, true answer to

their questions. They learned that when God is the response to every Why? When? and Where?, our questions really do get answered.

Surrounded by a great cloud of witnesses

When I found out that my uncle had cancer, I cried and cried. "Why, God? Why does it have to be Uncle Dale?" I was hurting for him. But when I first saw him it was so clear that he was at peace. He was not angry or bitter. He was calm and told me, "Yes, I am walking through the valley, but I will not be afraid. God is with me. He knew this was going to happen long before I did." I was amazed at his strength and his faith in God!

Friends and family were not the only ones with many more questions than answers. Dale, too, asked, "Why is this happening?" He discovered that people all over the world are suffering, have difficult situations. "Heartache and pain," he said, "like joy and success, are just part of life." But, God is part of life, too. In fact, He **is** life!

Dale wasn't angry at God. When I looked at Dale's life and his influence and asked, "Why did he get cancer?" I knew his focus was on loving Christ and the disease wouldn't stop him from continuing to invest in people. He loved people so intensely, and that's what I want to be true of my life, too.

A sure hope, despite an uncertain future

Dale was confident that God was working for his good, even though the cancer wasn't a good thing. He knew that suffering is part of our lives and is not surprising to Him.

NO, WE don't know what the future holds. Percentages and chances are man's way of making sense of the mystery of the future. We do know that my body withstood the aggressive treatment in a miraculous way. We know there were thousands of faithful saints around the world who have been praying. We know the results of the treatment have been all we could hope for.

What is around the corner is in God's hands. We are to walk by faith. It does appear that God has put more drops in the bucket of my life and I am the steward of what those drops get poured out on - it is to have eternal significance.

Many people asked God (and themselves), "Why Dale? Why cancer? Why him, of all people?" Ruby's answer, both honest and powerful, illustrates her great faith in God and strong love for her husband:

People have said that Dale and I are very close to something incredible: a complete transformation, where God refines the common, unattractive metal of our pain into the indescribable, incandescence of gold!

God has set this time apart for Dale and for me and it is a time we won't get to do over. For me, will I be completely here? To care for and support my beloved husband through the next unknown steps? There won't be any second chances. I am learning to surrender to God in each moment, to live fully in the reality of that particular time.

There is no promise that I will be happy, but I'm learning that my fears and pain can be transmuted into an inner peace and serenity that comes from a very deep place – the peace of God which passes all understanding.

Philippians 4:6-7 commands us, "Be anxious for

NOTHING; IN EVERYTHING GIVE THANKS, FOR THIS IS THE WILL OF GOD CONCERNING YOU. AND THE PEACE OF GOD WHICH PASSES ALL UNDERSTANDING WILL GUARD YOUR HEARTS AND MINDS…" *Compared to God's peace, my personal happiness is quite shallow.*

TO CALL this a time of testing our faith would be an understatement! Obviously, we don't question our eternal destiny with the Lord or our Christ-focused hope. But our human desire is to want to know what happens next, to see around the next corner in our path.

Imagining that I might not be in the next Christmas picture. Realizing that my time with Ruby, our sons and four grandsons might be coming to an end on this earth – that's tough.

Our hope and our trust, however, are in God! Every day has plenty of room for joy and thankfulness. We are blessed, so much so that letting it all go is not easy.

I sometimes ask Him for an easier path for me and my family, and His answer is always, "My strength is sufficient for you." So we abide in the presence of the One who loves us, knowing that cancer cannot separate any of us from His love which is in Christ Jesus!

A REALITY that continues to sink in that this will most likely be an unending battle until the Lord brings it to His closure. A closure that includes His refinement completed in my life.

The outer man is decaying, yet the inner man is being renewed day by day. We have plenty to be joyful for in the midst of uncertainty—plenty to be joyful for as we consider that the sting of death has been eradicated by the cross and the faithfulness of Christ.

Again, we must abide. There is no other option. We can't walk this road in our own strength, but in the arms of our Savior, we can. It's there, abiding in Him, that we find peace and safety, even though our earthly future is unknown.

I've been asked if I'm losing hope for a cure, and the answer is, "No!" Although now, more than ever, I know the true, lasting cure is from God alone. I will pursue all the medical regimens that the doctors prescribe and will receive them with the hope that they will be effective. However, fully cleansing my body of this cancer will take the divine medical skill of the Great Physician. The One who has known me before I was born, who loves me, delivers me, saves me and heals me.

The fire that refines...and enables

AS CRAZY as it might sound, I pray for the heat, the sense of complete dependency that comes when God turns on His refiner's fire. It is the fire that can produce holiness as we are yielded to His purposes. That kind of fire will cause an acute need for His abiding presence.

A significant challenge is maintaining a deep sense of need for Him, not just when I'm in the valley of the shadow of death but also when the still waters and green pastures are so comfortable.

These are the steps God has called me to take in obedience and trust as I walk His path in times when cancer isn't winning the battle:

• First, I must praise my God for the times of relief from pain. He has given a respite to me and to my wife and family as a temporal blessing.

• Second, I must remember that my life and time on this earth (like everyone's life, with or without cancer) is terminal. My days are numbered and I choose to live them in high definition. Even without the immediate terror of spreading disease I must maintain a mindset that clearly sees the things that have eternal value. And, the things that do not.

- Third, obedience, love, and faithfulness are not things that can be put off until tomorrow. Rejoicing always and praying without ceasing must begin now, or they will never happen. My obedience to God can't wait for the trigger of fear.

- Fourth, my life is not my own. I have been called and saved according to God's own mercy and grace. This life I live is His life and I pray that Christ will be exalted whether by life or by death. He gives me divine appointments every day. Will I accept them? More critical, will I carry them out?

THE LORD is my Shepherd – and so much more. I hunger for the spiritual passion that complete dependency creates, walking by faith and enjoying my Lord. Even when the valley does not appear to include the shadows of death, I want to be found holding His hand when the shadows do come.

Recalling the Good Shepherd's provisions for me, as seen in Psalm 23, Jesus anoints my head and continues to overflow my cup of blessing. As we finish our meal together, He

---

"As crazy as it might sound, I pray for the heat, the sense of complete dependency that comes when God turns on His refiner's fire. It is the fire that can produce holiness as we are yielded to His purposes. That kind of fire will cause an acute need for His abiding presence."

looks at me with love and compassion and says, "It is time to get on the trail again." He takes my hand and leads me back to the valley filled with shadows of death.

As I look up at the trail ahead, I see it is rough and steep, rising to a point I cannot see. My Savior says, "Follow Me. Place your feet where I place mine." I follow His footsteps as we climb. His presence lights our way through the shadows of darkness. I am not afraid.

I CAN'T remember the number of times I led groups of teens backpacking into the wilderness or on a biking adventure into Canada. In the midst of our day, regardless of wind, rain, steep terrain, or baking sun, we would always stop for lunch. Sometimes our meal would be on a grassy spot by the side of the road, by a lake, a rocky outcropping in the Mt. Jefferson Wilderness, or on a ferry between islands in British Columbia.

At the end of our meal we always gathered in a circle, opened God's Word and talked of His blessings, His plans for us, and our purpose in living. After that I'd say, "Two minutes to blast off!" and we'd continue our journey.

I led the group and they trusted me because I had been on the trail or road or waterway before. They followed in faith because they knew I truly cared about each one of them. How much more does our Heavenly Father care for each of us! That is why I can follow Him today, in the midst of uncertainty.

DURING THIS season of testing I'm learning the importance of focus. If we focus on the things we cannot do, we may never do the things we can. I may no longer be physically able to lead backpack trips, but I can teach younger leaders the essentials of wilderness camping. I can't run marathons now, but I can encourage, support, and give water to those who do. My physical body is rapidly declining but my inner man is being renewed every day.

God is giving me a can-do list that is keeping me very busy. Like last Sunday, when I hobbled to the pulpit with my swollen knees and they brought a stool for me to sit on. With God's enabling, I was able to teach from the Word.

Hebrews 12:3-13 has given me great comfort and instruction, especially regarding suffering. Verse 3 tells us to consider what Jesus endured; He is our frame of reference when it comes to adversity and suffering. That is why we are told to "...not grow weary and lose heart."

The passage ends with the word "therefore."

"THEREFORE, STRENGTHEN THE HANDS THAT ARE WEAK AND THE KNEES THAT ARE FEEBLE."

And I have a pair of very feeble knees right now! God allows and even designs the discipline of adversity for our good and for His holiness. Suffering in our lives is not a surprise to Him. I have heard Him say to me through His Word, "Dale, pick up your hands; don't be weak in the knees; fix your eyes on Jesus as you take My path straight to the cross."

The Apostle Paul prayed three times that his "thorn in the flesh" would be taken from him, but God's answer was "MY POWER IS PERFECTED IN WEAKNESS" (2 CORINTHIANS 12:9). In my weakness I have found amazing strength and purpose. He has never - and will never - ask more of me than He is willing to provide through His love, mercy, grace, and power.

THERE HAVE been ups and downs as the cancer has moved from my lungs to my brain; and then to my back; returning to my brain; and back again to my lungs. My cancer and the treatments have caused me more new kinds of aches and pains than I could have imagined.

These afflictions as well as a thousand others of this life

can cause us to be tossed around emotionally, spiritually, and mentally, like a stick in the waves. Nevertheless, I know He holds my hand as He calms the sea of my emotions, brings stillness to my spirit, and calms the fickle winds of my mind.

Whether this will be a long journey or a short one, we believe it is what the Lord has for us. Embracing the fire is the ongoing struggle that lies before us. Please pray that nothing will distract us from the firm hope we have in Christ. "THIS HOPE WE HAVE AS AN ANCHOR OF THE SOUL, A HOPE BOTH SURE AND STEADFAST." HEBREWS 6:19

God's strength is sufficient, enabling Ruby and I to walk each day in His faith and hope, regardless of how we feel or what we think. "MY FLESH AND MY HEART MAY FAIL, BUT GOD IS THE STRENGTH OF MY HEART AND MY PORTION FOR-EVER." PSALM 73:26

Imprinting lives, changing perspectives

"THEREFORE, SINCE WE ARE SURROUNDED BY SUCH A GREAT CLOUD OF WITNESSES, LET US ALSO LAY ASIDE EVERY WEIGHT, AND SIN WHICH CLINGS SO CLOSELY, AND LET US RUN WITH ENDURANCE THE RACE THAT IS SET BEFORE US, LOOKING TO JESUS, THE AUTHOR AND PERFECTER OF OUR FAITH, WHO FOR THE JOY THAT WAS SET BEFORE HIM ENDURED THE CROSS, DESPISING THE SHAME, AND IS SEATED AT THE RIGHT HAND OF THE THRONE OF GOD." HEBREWS 12:1-2

One of Dale and Ruby's friends sent them a quote, saying it applied especially well to Dale's attitude about life and about death: "Life is not a journey to the grave, with the intention of arriving safely in a pretty and well-preserved body. But, rather, to slide in broadside, thoroughly used up, totally worn out, and loudly proclaiming - man, what a ride!" People continued to write and send encouragements.

Dale, the way you keep going with a positive attitude, not complaining about your pain, that's what really stands out to me. I know you read God's Word with complete faith and trust, because it contains His will for your life. Even though it's hard for many of us to accept what is happening to you, you have accepted – even embraced – the path you are on, despite the debilitating pain.

It was hard for people to watch Dale and Ruby go through the cancer. Excruciatingly hard. It didn't matter if they were family and close friends or acquaintances living thousands of miles away, those praying for and hearing about the Prices' journey were deeply affected.

The often-repeated proverb, "Adversity does not build character, it reveals it," certainly applied to Dale. More than that, the cancer ordeal revealed, to an even greater degree, Dale's relationship to Christ.

Dale began every day by asking, "How can I live for Christ today?" As he became weaker his resolve grew stronger and we heard him say, "If I only could do more...." He ministered to others who had similar fates, to the doctors and nurses that cared for him, and continued with his ministry at Canyonview.

This has been Dale's way, as long as I've known him, when obstacles appear in his road. He wasn't satisfied with just sitting on the sidelines, waiting for the cancer to do its destructive work.

"He has never - and will never - ask more of me than He is willing to provide through His love, mercy, grace, and power."

Not at all. He and his family searched out the best doctors and treatments, the facilities that would be most helpful, and the schedules that would allow him the most time with his family and his ministries.

He was a man of infinite determination and optimism. In the autumn of 2008, when he was given no more than six months to live, he refused to accept that prognosis. Instead, he set new goals for himself - and wound up living an additional two years beyond that initial prediction.

৯৶৯৶৯

He had to have suffered with all of the treatments – numerous MRIs and CAT scans, chemotherapy, radiation and the brain Gamma-Knife procedure twice. But despite all the pain, he never gave up and he continued ministering in churches, homes, camps, doctor offices, and meetings, wherever he could talk about God's work in his life. And, he spent precious time with his family, creating memories for his wife, children, and grandchildren. Memories that will last until Christ returns.

৯৶৯৶৯

When Dale came to Creswell, he was already well into his fight with cancer. He was a new friend in my life, a gift from God, and cancer was part of his life from the first moment I met him. But when he talked about the unexpected discovery of cancer, Dale was very clear with me: "This has not taken God by surprise."

৯৶৯৶৯

Here at Canyonview, Dale's been our only leader and seems to us to be irreplaceable.

Where will we find what only he could bring to the ministry? From God, of course, but our director's shoes won't be easy to fill. Dale left an imprint of God's work and His Word, not of Dale Price's work or his words. Thankfully, he left a firm footing for us to follow and build on, and I believe his legacy will make Canyonview stronger in the future.

కలకల

I know it sounds like a cliché, but Dale really was one of a kind. Loved everyone, never disliked anyone. Spent time teaching and helping, welcomed people's questions. He made you feel like you were the most important person in his world.

కలకల

It has been Dale's serving heart, effective leadership and godly teaching that caused people to fall in love with Canyonview. His love for kids and desire to see them grow in Christ shows up in everything the camp does now and will do in the days ahead.

కలకల

After the cancer diagnosis, he never wavered in his faith. This man who was so strong, capable and successful in his ministry and with his family wasn't in control. It was a new role and experience for him. He needed help with so much, but was willing to be transparent and vulnerable with those around him.

కలకల

I have seen you go through major trials and tribulations due to the cancer. You have transparently made Scripture come alive and real to all of us. Scripture such as, "Even though I walk through the valley of the shadow of death, I will fear no evil" and "We walk by faith and not by sight." You have given me and thousands of others an example of what it means to truly follow in Christ's steps.

Dale's faith, as well as his enthusiasm for life, impressed me. The word "enthusiasm" means, literally, to be "filled with God," and Dale certainly was filled with God! He was always asking how others were doing and he truly waited to hear their answer. He cared deeply for his family and those around him.

When he lost his hair (due to chemotherapy) I had to share my favorite Bible verse with him, Luke 12:7: "Indeed the very hairs of your head are numbered. Don't be afraid; you are worth more than many sparrows."

Dale touched us all.

Primary-care nurse
Seattle Cancer Care Alliance

STEP BY STEP

Wednesday, December 17, 2008

On December 17, when we met with my doctors to find out the results of the CAT scan and blood work, God blessed us with amazing results. The radiologist reviewed my CAT scan and said the tumors showed, "Marked, marked, marked improvement since the initial CAT scan." In Dr. Martins' words, "The results are the best we could have expected."

The tumors have shrunk significantly and don't appear to be affecting my trachea. The tissue remaining in my lung does not appear to be cancerous. There is a chance that there may still be some cancer activity but the doctors are cautiously optimistic that there is not.

Our lives, as well as what is ahead, are in God's hands. In the meantime, we are to walk by faith. We are filled with thankfulness for God's grace and mercy.

Friday, March 6, 2009

Ruby and I just got home from Seattle last Tuesday night. The report from my oncologist was excellent. In his words, "We could not have gotten a better report. There is no sign of any cancer activity!"

My trachea is healthy and back to normal, and the scar tissue from the radiation is consolidating as expected. All my blood work is in the normal range. He even called me a "cancer survivor."

We know this is God's provision through the prayers of many. We also give thanks for the caring and skilled doctors who have been used by the Great Physician to accomplish this amazing result.

We continue to walk by faith on the path God has set before us. It is so exciting to watch His will unfold as we abide with Him on this journey.

May 14, 2009

Today I'm feeling the effects of what appears to be a big setback for us, in terms of the cancer battle.

About four weeks ago I had double-hernia surgery. Everything went well, but I was losing quite a bit of function in my left arm. We thought this might be due to a mini-stroke or pinched nerve.

When we came to Seattle for my regular check up, we were hoping for good news, like what we received this past December and March. We described the arm issues and suggested that the CAT scan include my neck. The CAT scan was followed by an MRI and both confirmed that the cancer had metastasized to my brain. The dysfunction in my left arm was a result of one of the five cancerous lesions they identified in my brain.

This updated diagnosis makes my new status, terminal. Treatment, if effective, may give us two to five years. If the cancer doesn't respond, then we're talking months, not years.

The course of treatment involves radiating the entire brain. These procedures started almost immediately and I have already had 12 of the 15 scheduled treatments. Next Tuesday we'll finish up and then wait a month for the next MRI to show us how the cancer has responded.

How are we doing?

First of all, thank you for your prayers and the many kind cards and letters. My body seems to be coping well with the treatment to aggressively deal with the tumors and shrink or destroy them. My headaches are gone and most of the function in my left arm is back. This is a hopeful sign that the cancer is responding to the treatment.

Wow! I've gone from cancer survivor in early March, to terminal cancer two months later. Discouraging, yes, but like Paul, "WE ARE HARD PRESSED ON EVERY SIDE, BUT NOT CRUSHED; PERPLEXED, BUT NOT IN DESPAIR; PERSECUTED, BUT NOT ABANDONED; STRUCK DOWN, BUT NOT DESTROYED." 2 CORINTHIANS 4:8-9

"I won't be defined by cancer. No! My identity is in Christ and His perfect plan."

Waterfall by Elaine Roemen

Chapter 4

Married in Ministry

"By God's grace, I will run this race God has set before me with the hope and courage you have come to count on. I will be a better man, husband, father, grandfather and friend because you have helped me put on God's armor, and have cheered me on as I have followed my Savior into the cancer battle.

"I will be forever thankful – how could I not be!!"

Dale and Ruby lived the biblical model for marriage. Two individuals join to become one. What God said to Adam and Eve in the Garden and Jesus echoed thousands of years later in Galilee, the Prices did for 40 years.

Their one-flesh marriage showed up in every part of their lives: family, ministry, relationships with others. And, during their cancer journey.

Because Ruby and Dale's marriage was built upon their relationships with God, their love-driven choices, and hard work, they received blessing upon blessing. Even more, their marriage blessed countless others as an example what a godly, real-world marriage looks and works like.

Celebrating a special milestone

RUBY AND I will be celebrating our 40th wedding anniversary on February 21, 2010. Because we don't know if the Lord will allow us a 50th celebration, we're going to make sure our 40th is something very special!

For the hundreds who turned out to honor the Prices at their 40th, it was an occasion to savor. Much more than an anniversary celebration, it was a chance to witness what God can do when two people who are willing to submit to Him and one another. Those listening as Dale and Ruby recited their renewed vows couldn't miss the depth and authenticity of their love for each other.

RUBY, I will always seek to bless you with my words and actions. I promise to build you up and encourage you to become all God wants you to be.

I will always endeavor to be your spiritual head. I will strive to love you as Christ loves the Church. I also promise to love you with the depth of human tenderness and affection that only God can inspire.

I will always seek to be understanding of you – your hopes, dreams, fears and struggles. I will share your burdens and your joys.

I will continue to expand the space for your adventurous spirit. Playing it safe is not for you! I want you to always run the race God sets before you with joyous abandon, knowing that my spirit is cheering you to the finish.

I will hold you and be by your side as long as God gives me breath. My touch will be there to comfort you and to keep you warm. Let that touch be a reminder of my faithfulness to you, and to our marriage.

I will laugh with you. I will seek to bring joy into every day, as we trust God with our fears. I will sing to you the love songs of my heart.

By God's grace, I will run this race God has set before me with the hope and courage you have come to count on. I will be a better man, husband, father, grandfather and friend because you have helped me put on God's armor, and have cheered me on as I have followed my Savior into the cancer battle.

I will be forever thankful – how could I not be!!

Love, Dale

*D*ale, I married the love of my life at age 19 and stand here today saying, "I would do it again!"

As we've traveled as partners in this journey of life, I have been blessed to be my captain's one and only first mate. As busy as you have been over the years, in your ministry to people, to your staff and campers, you always made time for your sons, and for me.

You demonstrated to a generation of Christian leaders that God can be No. 1 - in ministry, family and marriage.

You are a living example of how to be married in ministry.

Not only are you beloved by thousands who have expressed their appreciation for you during this past year, you are adored by your wife and deeply loved by your sons and daughters-in-law. They are paying you the highest of compliments by following in your footsteps. You are also beloved by your grandsons who, even though young, value your guidance and love spending time with you.

I will always bless you for giving me room to grow. You helped me envision possibilities beyond my experience, whether it was scuba diving, sailing in the Caribbean, or becoming a school principal and, then, district superintendent.

Most days you would leave me a note of encouragement, stuck to the coffee pot. I remember a particularly difficult stretch professionally, when things just weren't working out for me, when I found this note from you:

For however much time God gives us, I know that life with you will continue to be an amazing adventure. I promise to be arm-in-arm with you as we embrace the road before us. I will be your advocate, your encourager, your comforter, your lover, and dearest friend, for as long as God gives us breath.

I will continue to love, honor and respect you as the spiritual head of our home and family. When darkness threatens to overwhelm us, I promise to keep my eyes focused on the One who is Light. I will always be there for you, through weakness and strength, happiness and sadness, for better or worse. I will love you with every beat of my heart, forever.

Love, Ruby

WHEN I was diagnosed with cancer we didn't know if we would see our 40th anniversary. God continues to give me days of love and useful service. The phrase that seems fitting for this stage of my life is, "Cancer will not define my life but it will be used by God to refine it!"

That phrase came to me as I remembered our years of laughter and tears. I realized that our response to circumstances does not define who we are, it demonstrates who we are. As Peter's epistle puts it, "That the proof of your faith, being more precious than gold which is perishable, even though tested by fire, may be found to result in praise and glory and honor at the revelation of Jesus Christ."

A unique and godly relationship

The fact that Dale and Ruby's marriage was built on their shared faith in God and their desire to honor Him in all they did was plain to see. What was not as evident, at least to some, was how they lived out their marriage in the day-to-day of life.

Both of them were strong, motivated Christians with careers and ministries, two special people who pursued their callings with one another's respect and support.

They had a very open and supportive relationship in their marriage, even though some would have called it unconventional. Different enough that a few people asked questions about their decisions and actions. Why is Ruby working in another town than Dale? What does he really think about her career, since it isn't at the camp where he is?

But Dale supported Ruby at all times. They did everything in life together, including making decisions together. The difficulties they faced were worked out between them, no matter what it took or how long.

> *Ruby arrived with Dale for one of the prayer times the church's elders held for Dale after he got cancer. It was obvious that the information*

and emotions he shared with us were things they had already communicated with each other. I thought that was a very good indicator of the depth and strength of their relationship.

I met Ruby while she and Dale were dating and I was sure that she was the one for him. Dale and Ruby have honored each other and God throughout their married life and, as a result, they've become beloved role models to their children, friends, fellow Christians, and professional colleagues. Their relationships - with God, each other, their family and people in their ministries - always came first; things came second.

Ruby was close by Dale all the way, from their earliest days together, not just after he got cancer.

They weren't the typical Christian-marriage package, and their decisions sometimes didn't meet expectations others had for them. But unmet expectations didn't bother them.

One example is the Prices' move to Canyonview early in their marriage. To those who didn't know Dale and Ruby very well, the decision to pass on other opportunities and work with Ruby's father at a Christian camp that had barely begun was puzzling, to say the least. Ruby saw it differently:

I feel that I was the luckiest woman in the world to marry Dale and return to the camp. Even though I'd grown up there and not all my memories were positive, we weren't shackled by the past.

It was a great chance to create a different narrative and produce a brand-new story at Canyonview. The new work was a blessing, not only for our family, but for thousands in Christian ministry. That new story might be the greatest legacy we share as a couple.

Theirs was a very personal and practical marriage, and they thrived on what they had together. Dale and Ruby always listened to God and walked by faith, but they were also human, honest, and real. Between their public roles at Canyonview, the school district and church – not to mention in their cancer journey – Dale and Ruby were always visible to thousands.

> *I'm thankful God put Dale and Ruby Price in my life. The greatest impact Dale had on my life wasn't because of how he handled cancer. It was his devotion to Ruby that inspired me.*
>
> *In Creswell, Oregon, Dale was the lesser-known of the couple; the spotlight was on Ruby. She was not only the new school-district superintendent, she was our first-ever female in that role. The eyes of the media, along with everyone else's, were on Ruby Price, superintendent of schools for the Creswell School District.*
>
> *Dale? He was just her husband! I doubt that many people, outside of a few people in the*

> ✝ *There was wide ownership of Dale and Ruby as a couple, not just of their cancer situation. Hundreds of people beyond First Baptist Church wanted to be connected to the Prices, wanting to be involved in their lives. Just because of who they are.*

school district and the local pastors, really knew who Dale was. He was in the background. And that seemed to be just fine with Dale.

When we walked and talked, Dale spoke of his love for Ruby and his desire now, at this point in his life, to be her strongest supporter, her right-hand man, and her biggest fan as she pursued her calling in public education. It was OK with Dale to step away from the camp and have a minimal role there, moving to Creswell and serving in Ruby's shadow.

Dale was comfortable being who he was. And, at that time, being comfortable with himself also meant taking great pleasure in watching his wife be the professional/vocational/career leader in their marriage.

I have wondered if during his cancer experience, Dale experienced a course-correction spiritually regarding his support of Ruby. After so many years of him taking the lead with his ministry, he was seeing his wife ready, prepared, and eager to make a significant contribution to her profession and community. And, ultimately, to the cause of Christ.

One aspect of Dale's desire to become less as Ruby became more was his preparation for the future. In case he didn't win his battle with cancer and Ruby was left, he wanted to be certain she had every opportunity to succeed in her career and be known as much more than simply Mrs. Dale Price.

Dale's attitude perfectly reflected what John the Baptist said about his relationship with Jesus. "HE MUST BECOME GREATER; I MUST BECOME LESS" (JOHN 3:30).

It was quite an amazing thing for me to see. Dale chose to become less so Ruby could become more.

Dale's choices also modeled Paul's words in Ephesians 5. Paul says that husbands really love their wives when they give themselves up, just as Jesus loved the church and gave himself up for her.

We read that particular Scripture, agree with it and hear sermons preached on it, but we see it lived out very rarely. I am married to a schoolteacher who has many gifts, yet I must admit that I find it difficult to set aside my own ministry and personal ambitions for her.

Dale, however, demonstrated the kind of self-denial and sacrifices our Savior commanded and lived in His love for the church.

When it came to their careers and ministries (together as well as individually), the Prices charted their course together. No job or service was more important than their unity and their commitment to having a God-honoring marriage.

Both Dale and Ruby agonized over their decision for her to set aside her highly successful career as an educator to care for him full time. It was a tremendous sacrifice, but also a great comfort for them. The comfort came in knowing that they had considered the options, prayed, talked, and reached a joint decision.

Her care for him was amazing and she became a hero to me and my family as we watched her give and give and give some more. The circumstances were often overwhelming, but Ruby did it by relying on God's strength and her husband's love for her.

❦❦❦

People asked why Ruby didn't just quit her job the moment she found out about Dale's cancer. Or why she took a different job later on in the cancer journey. Maybe they missed or ignored the fact that Dale was the world's biggest fan and supporter of his wife's professional life. He knew how much she loved what she was doing; how good she was at it; and how it was such an important part of Ruby.

His unwavering support for her is yet another fantastic trait about Dale the husband; he valued his wife so much that whatever mattered to her mattered to him.

They both worked hard and put in long hours at their respective jobs, but Dale would always carve out time for just the two of them.

For better and for worse, but always for each other

Dale loved me unconditionally. His love for me and his attitude about what we were going through more than overcame our difficulties.

Although living with Dale's cancer had been a team effort for the Prices from the start, Ruby knew she wanted – and needed – to take a more active role in his care. Her desire to be with him as much as possible meant adjustments to her career and the need to communicate those changes to others.

Dale was so transparent with people. Letting people know what he was going through helped me take a very different approach to many things, including my professional life. Instead of continuing to just "put on the lipstick, smile and pretend everything was OK," I learned how to begin letting others into my personal ordeals.

When I explained my need to have an extended leave of absence so I could be with Dale, his example of forthrightness and honesty helped me speak to my colleagues boldly, even emotionally, and not feel like I had to pretend nothing was wrong.

Part of the cancer's huge impact on Ruby was the difficult and seemingly unending questions. For those times, Dale was there.

When I asked, "How can God allow such pain?" and "Who's going to take care of me if you're gone?" his support was my rock.

Dale was Ruby's anchor during those stormy times when she had real despair, even struggling to keep a tight grip on her faith. As she gained strength from her husband's strength, Ruby continued writing down her conversations with God and her thoughts about the road she was travelling, a practice she had begun in 2006.

I must do this, create a gratitude journal and add to it regularly. I am too focused on the losses I've experienced, too caught up in rejections and hurts, instead of recounting all the blessings God has poured into my life.

Each day I will find at least one thing to be grateful for. I'll begin by being thankful for my wonderful, supportive and loving husband, who has never stopped showing me how proud he is of me.

Dale and Ruby strove to always be transparent with each other, especially as the cancer worsened and questions nagged about how things would end. Although it wasn't always easy, temporarily setting aside their ministry and professional personas – camp director, school superintendent, workshop presenters, church leaders, etc. – and reaffirming their relationship and keeping first things first helped them stay in sync.

Dale said he was more in love with Ruby during his battle with cancer than at any other time. The reason, he explained, was that as their need for God increased and He sustained them, Dale gained a greater capacity to love his wife.

At the same time, Dale was saddened at the prospects for Ruby's future, should God choose to call him home before her. The thought of not being able to finish their earthly journey together was almost too much for him to bear. His only comfort was the certain knowledge that God would carry his beloved Ruby through whatever storms and valleys came her way, as He had faithfully done all their lives.

"You're the one dying," Ruby told Dale once. "Yes," replied Dale, "but you're the one living. I'll be in my heavenly home with my eternal Father, but you will still be here." Dale's grief was sudden and deep when he thought of having to leave his lifelong partner, possibly very soon.

In one of his special notes to Ruby, Dale found yet another way to express his everlasting love to his wife:

DEAREST RUBY,

I love you.

But before you read any further, I want you to open the gift attached to this letter. Open, open, open!! Now, don't read the rest of this letter yet. I mean it!

(**Editor's note**: *Turn to the next page now to see the gift.*)

Storm by Elaine Roemen

a present for Ruby

NOW, FOR the rest of this note:

When I first saw this painting I was struck by many things. Its power and its beauty, of course. But as I have dreamt about it, deeper thoughts and feelings have emerged.

I see two of God's creatures running, for the sheer joy of running, but they are running together. Although the storm clouds boil in the background and the vision of the sea isn't quite clear, they run as one through the fields of God.

Lately, you have said, "We're not sleep-walking through life," and I agree.

Imagine that those two beautiful horses are a vision of us and our life together. There is the strange mixture of fear, wonder and excitement in their run across the grassy bluff. There is a storm in the distance and with an unseen goal ahead they run.

Because they are together, there is comfort for their fears and a shared joy and wonder as they romp through creation. Exhilarated delight shines in every movement as they race as one toward a shared destiny.

I love you, my beautiful wife, friend, and lover. I will love you forever; I will love you for always. Thirty-seven years is just part-way toward our shared destiny.

Love, Dale

They learned to live one day at a time, doing their best to avoid thinking of the what-if, concentrating on the right-now. Dale and Ruby talked things over, checking in with each other regularly to find out what the other was learning on their painful and always-changing journey. Discovering where their spouse needed an extra prayer or loving touch.

We try to be strong for each other, but we want to

be completely honest, too. That meant plenty of tears, of course, but we didn't get stuck there for too long.

No matter what was going on with Dale's health, in the lives of their family and friends, or in their ministry and career worlds, they always returned to their foundation: Abiding and trusting in God.

The likely loss of what Dale and Ruby had looked forward to for years was especially difficult. Like most anyone, they had their "bucket list," the people, places, and activities they'd planned making part of their retirement years. Spending more time with the grandkids, short-term missions, travelling, building a house of their own... Now, these represented unfulfilled dreams, missed possibilities and lost futures.

But the greatest loss they were contemplating was that which was most dear and entirely irreplaceable - Dale.

The thing is, I'm losing my husband. Sure, seeing hopes and dreams for careers and houses and recreation dissolve is hard, but those losses are nothing compared to losing Dale.

People question me about facing the very real possibility that Dale will be gone soon. "How do you do it, Ruby?" they ask. And I tell them, "I don't really do 'it' at all. It's too much for me to handle by myself. Without the Lord I'd be completely without hope."

Dale's cancer was a huge shock for Ruby, but it also drew her closer to God. One result of that intensified dependence on God was a closer relationship with Dale. She has grieved deeply and will grieve even more in the days ahead, but the pain won't be wasted. Ruby's love for the Lord and for Dale will be used by God to strengthen her in ways that will both heal her and touch others like never before.

Two people, one marriage, touching many

Hello Dale and Ruby, I prayed for you today, that God would hold you in the palm of His hand, so you can say with the psalmist, "You are my hiding place, You will protect me from trouble and surround me with songs of deliverance."

I know your battle is hard right now. You have been such an inspiration to me, leading me to have more faith and help me see my troubles as small in comparison with yours.

ക്ക്ക

*I prayed Psalm 91:4 for you today. "*He will cover you with his feathers and under his wings you will find refuge; his faithfulness will be your shield and rampart.*"*

ക്ക്ക

Dale, I really want you to know how much you have meant to me. I have looked to your guidance, reassurance and a godly example of an earthly father should be like. Your counsel has made a real impression on me. Thank you for touching my life and the lives of many others.

ക്ക്ക

Dale hired me to work at Canyonview as a horse-camp counselor (something I knew absolutely nothing about!) and I became good friends with his son, Matt. Over time, Dale and Ruby became like parents to me and have been big supporters of me, even contributing to my financial support while I served in missions in Africa for four years. When I returned to the U.S. in 2006, I came back to camp and became very close to both Ruby and Dale.

I'm so grateful for how both of them invested in me professionally and spiritually, and helped me see what kind of a man I could be (and hope to be).

᳒᳒᳒

The thread that's carried through all the years is the Prices' faith in God and the role models they provided for me. Their marriage and the quality of their character as individuals is what drew me to them in the first place. So warm, nurturing, positive, growing. They didn't have fairytale life, but I knew it was real and it was because of God.

*Hebrews 13:7 says, "*REMEMBER THOSE WHO LED YOU, WHO SPOKE THE WORD OF GOD TO YOU; AND CONSIDERING THE RESULT OF THEIR CONDUCT, IMITATE THEIR FAITH.*"*

The Prices let God use them in my life and in the lives of so many others. Dale gave me guidelines on how to live healthy and how to handle the changes that came my way. Dale and Ruby always spoke the truth, but did it without judging people or making them feel insignificant.

I thank God that He gave me the best, Dale and Ruby. He knew what - and who - I needed in order to grow up, to come into a real relationship with God.

᳒᳒᳒

I am impressed by Ruby's honesty and vulnerability as she waits on the Lord with Dale. Her devotion to Dale is obvious – not only as his wife, but as one who shares his passion

*to manifest Christ as they respond to the good
and bad developments in Dale's cancer. They've
found some incredibly positive ways to redeem
the time God has granted them.*

A marriage that was blessed...to bless others

Many times over the years, Dale and Ruby presented several highly regarded workshops, including "Married in Ministry" and "Building Strong Marriages." Their audiences included camp directors, pastors, church staff, young marrieds and leaders from parachurch organizations. It didn't matter if you had been married for 45 years or 45 days, or your ministry touched a dozen or thousands, the Prices were always able to impart God's truth, while encouraging, challenging, and blessing those who attended.

> **ONE REASON** we started doing the workshops and seminars was because people kept asking us about our relationship, how we parented, and how to make it all work in a ministry context. We'd get questions like, "Your marriage is obviously thriving, even though you're super-involved at camp, in your church, with your kids, and more. How do you do it?" and "How do you handle it when people _____ (fill in the blank)?"

The Prices lived what they taught and modeled what they spoke to the seminar participants. They believed God had called them to share with others what they'd learned in 40 years of marriage and 35 years of full-time ministry experience.

In addition to the coaching and counseling opportunities they did with individuals, couples and families near their home base, God was made it clear that they needed to take their knowledge and experience on the road. He wanted them to go to other places, including overseas, to reach people who were hurting and struggling to succeed both in their marriages and their ministries.

Their seminars and workshops covered a number of foundational and practical topics, such as:

• How To Keep Your Relationship Fresh And Thriving In The Ministry Fishbowl.

• Can Marriage and Ministry Cohabitate?

• A Cord of Two Strands Is Not Quickly Torn Apart: The Dynamics of a Healthy Marriage in the Ministry Environment.

• The Secret Trauma Of Ministry Marriages: Where Can The Walking-Wounded Go For Help And Who Can They Trust?

• The Myth Of The Perfect Ministry-Marriage, Family And Home.

• Godly Marriages Chart The Course To Our Genuine Joy And Contentment.

• Husbands And Wives (And Their Marriages) Are To Be Examples Of Process, Not Perfection.

One of Dale and Ruby's most popular handouts came from their "Building Strong Marriages – Yours and Theirs" seminar. Their main point was, "If our commitment to each other is greater than our problem, we will always solve our problem; if our problem is greater than our commitment, the problem wins." After apologizing for taking great liberties with Paul's instructions from 1 Corinthians 13:1-3, Dale proceeded to stress the importance of valuing one's marriage and family over one's ministry (including his own):

If I speak with words that light the fire in a hundred young hearts,
If I lead singing and play guitar at nightly campfires,
But lose my family
I have become a noisy gong or a clanging cymbal.

And if I have the gift of leadership,
And know all aspects of my ministry's operations,
And have all faith so as to regularly meet my budget,
But lose my family
I am nothing!

And if I give all my possessions to the ministry,
And regularly burn the midnight oil,
And get burned out in the process,
But lose my family
I have lost everything!

"The outer man is decaying, yet the inner man is being renewed day by day. We have plenty to be joyful for in the midst of uncertainty—plenty to be joyful for as we consider that the sting of death has been eradicated by the cross and the faithfulness of Christ."

STEP BY STEP

May 21, 2009

Ruby and I arrived back in Port Orford last night. I finished my course of 15 whole-brain radiation treatments on Tuesday. Apart from the radiation burn on my head, some headaches and overall weakness, I survived it pretty well. The doctors are very hopeful.

I also started a gene-therapy pill which targets the specific cancer cells of the type I have and inhibits their growth. We'll return to Seattle in a month for a CAT scan on my lungs and an MRI on my brain. We are all praying for a good result and that the Lord will prolong my physical life according to His purpose.

Meanwhile we live life in high definition. We are blessed every day and every encounter with another person is a divine appointment.

Two recent blessings stand out:

1.   After arriving in Seattle for radiation treatment No. 14, we drove to the Marriott Hotel on Lake Union expecting our standard (cancer-patient-special) room. instead, we found that the manager had upgraded us to a lake-view, two-bedroom suite (which goes for $600 per night) at no extra cost!

2.   We went to dinner later and squeaked in one minute before the end of the half-price Early Bird Special. After ordering, we had the opportunity to share our story with our waitress. She proceeded to bring her manager over, so we could talk again about our faith and trust in God. Sharing the Good News of God's faithfulness is reward enough, but we received a double portion of blessing when the manager brought over two servings of the restaurant's famous and gigantic banana cream pie - at no charge!

June 2, 2009

The past couple of weeks I've been working through some serious radiation burn on my head. I think my whole head has peeled four times, including under my eyelashes and in my ear canals! While dealing with that discomfort, my strength continued to fade and my left arm began losing its functionality.

Thanks to God's grace, the head-peeling has stopped. And thanks to the efforts of my kind doctors (each one is a gift from God), the use of my left arm is 90-percent restored. The next MRI, set for June 22, should tell us how the cancer is responding to treatments. I believe the results will be good, based on how I'm feeling now.

I've spent some quality time with Ruby down on the southern coast of Oregon. I was honored to give the baccalaureate address to the graduating seniors in Ruby's school district. It was a privilege to share my faith, as well as telling them how and why the most important growth doesn't happen in the green pastures and still waters of life.

Sharing from 2 Peter 1:3-8 and 1 Timothy 4:12, I tried to help these young adults understand the power that matures us personally and spiritually. That force is the Refiner's fire, God's work in our lives when we are tested. This opportunity, like so many others the Lord has divinely appointed, would not have happened without my having had cancer. Talk about redeeming the time!

June 24, 2009

We know many of you have been praying as we approached the next round of tests. Thank you for holding our lives up to the Father in prayer. He is sustaining us.

We arrived in Seattle on Monday in time for the MRI on my brain and the blood work. At our appointments the next day, the doctors were pleased with the results. The five cancerous lesions (discovered in April) have responded well to the whole-brain radiation treatment. They are not gone, but they have all shrunk, some more than others. Yes, we all had hoped the tests would show the cancer in my brain was eradicated, but that was not the Lord's will – not yet anyway.

Nevertheless, we have exciting news! My doctors cleared me for a procedure called "gamma knife," an aggressive treatment which specifically targets cancer sites in the brain.

We're very encouraged, not only because the gamma knife may eliminate the cancerous lesions, but because the amount of cancer in my brain would normally disqualify me from consideration for this treatment. Gamma knife is usually used only when three or fewer (not the five I have) lesions are present. Fortunately, my overall health and past tolerance of aggressive treatment puts me in the "possible" category. The gamma-knife procedure is scheduled for next Tuesday and will take the entire day. I have also been on a gene-therapy regimen for about 35 days now, and am tolerating the side effects well.

We are blessed by a team of doctors who truly care and want the best for us. Dr. Rockhill, the gamma-knife expert and newest member of the team, joins Dr. Patel (radiation oncologist) and Dr. Martins (lung-cancer oncologist). Pray for these men who have been placed in our lives to minister their skills to us. We have been placed in their lives to be the aroma of Christ among them and live lives of love, faith, and trust in the midst of the Refiner's fire.

We're doing OK. The outer man is decaying, yet the inner man is being renewed day by day. We have plenty to be joyful for in the midst of uncertainty—plenty to be joyful for as we consider that the sting of death has been eradicated by the cross and the faithfulness of Christ.

July 1, 2009

Well, the big day is over and I'll try to describe the hours we spent at Harborview Medical Center undergoing the gamma-knife procedure.

After Ruby and I got back from Victoria, B.C., yesterday evening (I'll tell more about that blessing later), we asked the front desk to give us a 5:30 a.m. wake-up call so we could be at the hospital by 6:30 a.m.

Here is a rough sequence of the day's events:

• 6:30 a.m. – As the I.V. is hooked up we fill out medical and liability releases, and other paperwork.

• 7 - Meet with Dr. Goodkin, an oncology expert and someone who's experienced in the fitting of the gamma-knife frame. He explains the risks and benefits to us.

• 7:30 – We begin by putting the titanium frame on my head, numbing four spots on my head (two on my forehead and two on the back of my head), and carefully adjusting the frame so that the tumor sites can be reached by the radiation without hitting the frame itself. Then the frame is attached to my skull by sharp pins that are screwed through the frame and into my skull. This is necessary to make sure my head doesn't move during the procedure.

• 8:30 - My first MRI of the day.

• 9 - Start of the gamma-knife procedure. Radiation is shot through 201 separate holes to focus on each of the tumor sites. The four radiation sessions last from 7 to 23 minutes, and they have to reset the machine after each session. The fifth tumor cannot be reached with this frame setting, so they have to remove the frame from my head.

- 12:30 - Start setting up for the new frame mounting on my head, complete with four new owies as new pins are placed in new spots.
- 1:30 - New MRI using the new frame.
- 2:30 - Start of the final gamma-knife treatment.
- 3:30 - Debriefing by the doctors as the frame is removed. Possible side effects are reviewed again, which include possible seizures for the next 48 hours, headaches, pain at the sites of the screw pins, etc.
- 4:30 - Leave the hospital.

We wouldn't normally recite such a detailed account of my treatment, but so many of you have asked, we wanted to give you some idea of our day. It was a day of great hopefulness. Coupling the gamma knife with the whole-brain radiation has proved to be very effective for many patients.

This business of trusting - in the skills and procedures of the best doctors we can find, in God to work through them, and in the prayers of thousands of people - is challenging spiritually. Our faith is in God and His power to heal. The preservation of my life for five hours or for five years won't happen apart from the work of the Great Physician.

As promised earlier, I must tell you about an amazing and blessed mini-vacation Ruby and I had recently. We knew we wanted to get away and had to stay within a couple hundred miles of Seattle, but weren't sure where to go.

Although Ruby and I had led many bike and sailing trips to and through Victoria, an hour and a half north of Seattle, we had not visited there as a couple in 30 years. When I found a half-price room was available at the magnificent Empress Hotel, our minds were made up.

We had a beautiful room on the sixth floor for the first two nights. Then, a very kind man on the front desk voluntarily upgraded us (at no expense) to a one-bedroom corner suite on the fourth flour. We were so blessed! We slept in, walked, prayed, ate out at new restaurants, and explored the southwest coast of Vancouver Island.

July 24, 2009

After our drive to Seattle on Sunday, we spent Monday getting tests, both the MRI (on my brain) and a CAT scan (over the entire body).

On Tuesday we got some difficult news from all three of my oncologists. A mass appears to be growing near my esophagus and they found two new spots on my brain. Although the spots were small, it was a sign that the whole-brain radiation hadn't been as effective as we had hoped.

On Wednesday I had a PET scan. It is like a CAT scan, covering the entire body, but radioactive material is injected to show any active cancer sites.

Then, on Thursday, we met with my radiation oncologist, Dr. Patel, and my primary oncologist, Dr. Martins, to find out what the PET scan revealed. Thankfully, the mass near my esophagus is not cancerous. Of concern, however, is the presence of two active cancer sites. Neither of these had been identified previously. The scan also showed cancer activity in one of the bones of my left hip and my left lung (in one of the tumors we had previously treated with chemo and radiation).

My doctors are unsure if the cancer-cell growth in my lung and hip are recent. The activity could have happened either before or after I started the Tarceva gene-therapy treatment. (Tarceva works to control cancer growth but does not necessarily kill it.)

What my doctors want me to do is to continue using Tarceva and do all I can to stay strong and healthy. They'll look me over in another month.

So we continue to walk by faith, with our Lord - who is always faithful. Although we were not encouraged by my test results, the doctors emphasized that it could have been much worse. The PET scan could have shown many more cancer sites. I could also be showing debilitating results from the brain cancer and/or its treatment. And

---

"What has kept me strong throughout this challenging year is knowing and living in His truth, that in Him is light and no darkness at all. When darkness closes in, I look to my Light and find plenty of hope - for today and tomorrow."

---

they have more tools in their arsenal that they have not yet used.

I am striving to discern God's long-term plan in all this, yet I know that His life-design is perfect. I am a blessed man who can truly say, there is nothing that can separate me from the love of God in Christ Jesus. Neither life, nor death, nor any created thing. Romans 8:38-39 (very loosely paraphrased)

August 21, 2009

Thank you for all your prayers and notes of encouragement.

Of all the symptoms I've been through, the nausea I am experiencing seems the most debilitating. Let me say that I now have great empathy for any woman who has ever had morning sickness! Mine, however, is morning, noon, and night. The look, smell or taste of almost any food is enough to send me running to the sink. I'm trying medications that may provide some relief. I've lost too much weight, and I'm trying to compensate with protein drinks, oatmeal, and fresh fruit.

September 20, 2009

Many of you have heard that my father, Dr. Nelson C. Price, passed away last Sunday, September 13, at the age of 91. He did not suffer long, and when the Lord called him home, he was surrounded by those who loved him.

He and I talked nearly every day these past couple of years. He was very concerned about my health and checked in on me all the time. I still have his last message to my cell phone. "How are you feeling, buddy?" is what my loving, earthly father said.

September 24, 2009

I am writing from our hotel overlooking Lake Union in Seattle, on the day we got the results of my latest tests. The doctor's report was a mixture of good news and bad news. It wasn't all we had hoped for, but there is still much that keeps us hopeful. The stress of not knowing the test results was very hard, so now we have a much better idea of what we are dealing with.

Let's start with the bad news.

The cancer that showed up in my tests a month ago in my sacrum (center part of the pelvic bone) is still there and is showing increased activity, enough so that the doctor was surprised I wasn't in more pain. (Lately I've been managing with ibuprofen and Tylenol.)

As a result of this increased cancer activity, Dr. Martins prescribed more chemotherapy to address the cancer's spread. My first treatment was today. We'll go through a couple of the one-hour treatment cycles every three weeks, and then take another CAT scan to determine the effectiveness of the treatment. Please pray that the chemo will be effective.

Now, for the good news!

The PET scan didn't show any new areas of cancer growth. None in my lungs or anywhere else. Praise God!

October 12, 2009

Over the last few weeks I have been blessed by an increasingly good appetite and a decrease in the pain in my lower back.

I initially attributed the decrease in pain to the Tylenol 3 I was taking. But because I have been able to significantly reduce the amount of pain medications I am taking, I believe the chemo is having a positive effect. I give thanks to our God for the thousands of you who remember us in prayer regularly. God is answering your prayers as we walk this road of faith.

October 23, 2009

Ruby and I just got back home from Seattle. The doctors were pleased with my blood work, my weight and my reduced pain. They said the lessening of the pain was the best indicator that the chemo is working. The steroids they gave me with the chemo kept me going for two days, but then I lost energy.

During our appointment with Dr. Martins, I asked about the chemo's effectiveness.

"Will the chemotherapy I've been having completely do away with my cancer? Is it even possible that the chemo can even cure me?"

"No, Dale, your cancer won't be cured by the chemo treatments. You need to figure out how to live out the days you have left as fully as possible."

Although I had already heard this prognosis before, the words were still hard to receive. Other doctors estimated that I had one to three years to live, and their words rushed back into my mind.

A great sadness came over me, not because I feared death or questioned the eternity that God has prepared for me. No, I was sad because I was clinging to my life and identity as Ruby's husband; as father to Josh and Matt and to my daughters-in laws Jennifer and Amy; as grandfather to Tyler, Cody, Noah, and Logan; as Buzzard at Canyonview; and as one who loves my family and friends.

October 26, 2009

A few of you expressed concern after reading my last update, and I want to talk about how Ruby and I are feeling after those disappointing conversations with the doctors.

Yes, their words indicating that my cancer is incurable were hard to hear. But as I said in that update and have been saying for as long as I've been a Christian, God is the only one who knows my days. There may not be any medical hope for a long life, but that does not mean I am without hope.

What has kept me strong throughout this challenging year is knowing and living in His truth, that in Him is light and no darkness at all. When darkness closes in, I look to my Light and find plenty of hope - for today and tomorrow.

I feel great. Ruby and I are going to Willamette Valley Cancer Institute in Eugene today to see if I can get some of my chemo treatments there rather than needing to travel to Seattle every time.

I am preaching this Sunday at a local church in Creswell, thankful for every opportunity I have to share about God's faithfulness and what it means to truly walk by faith.

Mr. Price is a man of faith. The term "faith" is sometimes used rather loosely, but not in his case. He fights his lung cancer with his faith, a faith that says life has a purpose, even if we cannot always identify it. His courage in battling this terrible disease is grounded in his faith in God and in the love of his family.
University of Washington oncology doctor

Chapter 5

A Family United

"One of the hardest things for me has been realizing I'm not in control. I'm finding out what it means to really and completely give over control of my life (and the lives of those I love) to God. It's not my natural response when facing tough situations and it's not easy."

Few would disagree that growing up in a healthy family is one of the best gifts a child can receive. A person's family influences their future development more than nearly any other factor. The value of a family in which everyone is respected, loved, protected, challenged to grow and prepared to thrive outside the family can hardly be overestimated.

So, what does it take to build a family that does more than share the same last name or occupy the same mailing address? What is true about the members of families who are making a difference in the lives of the people around them?

Look to Dale and Ruby Price's family – and the ways it blessed others – for the answers.

Doing family together

Dale and Ruby were devoted to one another, and together they created a loving and godly home in which to raise their two sons, Joshua and Matthew. Even though both parents were involved with many ministries and countless relationships, the family remained their primary focus.

> *The ways in which Dale, Ruby and their family entered into the fight against cancer was amazing. His will to live, his love of life and love for his family allowed him to endure many challenging procedures. As months went by, then a year, and then two, it became harder to think of him as being so sick. He and Ruby, often with their family, went snowboarding, water skiing, scuba diving in Mexico, on speaking trips to Russia, and maintained an ongoing ministry to others. He was living his life instead of waiting to die.*

> *Dale found his comfort in his Savior and in continuing to do what he loved best: Love his family, minister to others, and be the best*

husband he could be for Ruby. Even at his sickest he would get up to be with his children, grandchildren and visitors. He struggled when others grieved for him and did all he could to encourage and comfort them.

∽⌒∽⌒∽⌒

My aunt and uncle are best friends and care deeply for each other. At the same time, they care just as much about others. They really pour their lives into one another and the people around them. They both have such large hearts - there's room for many people.

One time Dale and Ruby invited me and my kids to Sunriver with them, and treated my kids as their own grandkids. During that time my uncle slept a lot, but he still wanted to be with us, seeing kids playing and laughing. He was in a lot of pain and it was hard for him to be comfortable, but he didn't complain.

But for Uncle Dale, life wasn't about being comfortable. As he saw things, life was about spending time together and building memories. Even though some of the most-recent memories were hard and others were probably coming to an end, he lived completely in high definition. He wasn't happy going through the fire of cancer, but he was willing. He had – and communicated – joy despite his pain.

My Aunt Ruby was a gracious caregiver to her beloved husband. As she grieved, however, she continued to believe that God would heal him if that was part of His plan. During that time she also made sure to take time to rejuvenate, staying active with things like ice skating with her grandchildren and walking.

Their influence on my life has been enormous.
They have counseled me in my personal walk
with Christ, my marriage and my parenting.

Passing the torch

Despite well-known (and sometimes accurate) clichés about similarities between children and their parents, the character traits and life decisions of sons and daughters often bear little resemblance to those of their parents.

The apple doesn't fall far from the tree. Chip off the old block. Like father, like son.

Spiritual matters are no different. Most parents hope their children will follow in the steps of faith they've tried to demonstrate, but there are no guarantees. Each child must find his and her own way, deciding who and what they'll follow, how they'll order their priorities, and the kind of marriage and family they want. Sometimes the results are very different from what those kids' parents lived and taught earlier.

And, sometimes, the children's faith, marriages, and families reflect quite accurately those of the parents.

Dale's been a great dad to his sons and they've turned out to be great fathers. Matt and Josh were very involved with Canyonview's ministry, co-leading trips and counseling. They even met their wives while serving at camp. It's been wonderful and very satisfying to watch our sons and their wives grow closer together as they grew concerned about Dale and his health.

ఈఈఈ

Dale and Ruby wanted to spend as much time as they could with our kids, even as Dale's condition got worse. But they've always been like that, looking for opportunities to read to the boys, watch movies, and take them places. Our sons idolized Dale – and they still do to this day – because he took the time to know them and love them.

We wanted them both to slow down more, but they were too involved, too active, and loved too many people! You would never know they were dealing with cancer. The treatments, Dale's near-constant pain, the dozens of trips to and from Seattle...none of that was as important to my husband's parents as loving people and serving God. They just didn't think about living at a different pace or cutting things and people out of their lives. I think those trips and activities, and definitely the people, helped keep them strong.

Another incredible thing was Dale and Ruby's complete acceptance and support of us, our marriage, and our family. They were always proud of us, trusted us and loved us (and they didn't tell us how to parent!).

৵ঙ৵ঙ৵ঙ

Passing the blessing to the next generation: bring up your kids for God's service

One of Dale and Ruby's most-popular seminars taught parents the necessary ingredients for creating a family that honored God and raised godly kids.

Glancing through the main points of their seminar outline below shows us what Dale and Ruby practiced while raising their own children.

•   Parents need to ask themselves (and answer!) the Number 1 question they face: What is the goal of our parenting?

•   Building a loving, godly family isn't a job for Dad and Mom do alone. Get the help our Father God offers – prayer, the Spirit, the Word, His people, the fruits of the spirit, and His armor.

- The Lord has given most of us a husband or a wife, with whom we can lead effectively.
- Make sure you and your spouse are united in spirit, in your thinking and in your purpose.
- Be intentional, personal, relational and real (remember, you are not perfect!) with your kids.
- Is the Word of God coming out of our mouths, being lived out in our lives?
- We choose to live lives based on God's value system, not someone else's.
- What does the Bible say about the role of parents in the lives of their grown children?
- Grandchildren are your kids' children, not yours! Grandparents, provide an example to your grandchildren, encourage them, and be available.

Mom and Dad's marriage: our model for family

I'm so thankful for my parents' walk with God, their love for each other and the way they raised us.

It's just been over the past few years that I've realized the huge blessing I've received being part of my family. My parents lived out their faith in real ways, with real people. It wasn't just a Sunday thing or a bunch of words they used around certain people. Their relationship with Christ showed up in everyday life.

Mom and Dad were an incredible team. Their love for each other – expressed in loving notes, words of affection and flowers going back and forth - has been inspiring. They cheered each other on; Mom with Dad's military and camp careers and Dad with her career in education as a principal and a superintendent.

My mom was really amazing spiritually, as well as in every other way. She was the perfect partner for my dad, planning family trips that took all four of us backpacking, biking, boating, and more. She was very adventurous, especially if the activity gave her a chance to try something for the very first time!

The other thing people need to know about Mom is her unconditional love. You don't have to be someone special or do anything to receive her generosity. She finds ways to love all the people around her, not just her family.

The overflow of God's love in my dad's life inspired me to be around him. He had such a strong appreciation of the Lord's creation on land and water and in the skies. I remember so many times I'd be backpacking with him, listening as he marveled at what God had done. I grew up with that same passion for creation, seeing and experiencing God through what He made. Dad's frequently shouted out, "Isn't God incredible!" always giving God credit for His handiwork and acknowledging Him as Almighty God. It wasn't an act or an attempt to show others how spiritual he was. That exclamation was just my dad's authentic response to what God had done and is doing.

Everything was an adventure with Dad! The way he lived was an amazing example to me, and he always focused on relationships over tasks.

Matt Price, Dale's son

At Dale's bedside, as he was dying, Matt and Josh were asked if they resented having had to share their dad with so many other people. They looked at each other in disbelief and said, "No! Dad was always 100 percent there for us."

It was pretty unique for us, growing up at camp. That was also where I began growing in my relationship with the Lord. I heard lots of Bible stories, praise songs, good teaching and stories. Even back then, when I was a kid, I knew that being at Canyonview Camp was a huge blessing. Having the parents I had, plus being part of something as cool and special as the camp, was great. And my dad was usually in the middle of it all!

I really began to know about God and follow Christ the year I worked as a junior counselor at Canyonview. I love that ministry of teaching and encouraging the campers. I served in many other roles at camp in high school and into my early college years. Although I was out from under my parents' wings at that time, I knew I wanted my life to count for the Lord.

With my parents, everything revolved around prayer. I saw them praying together, individually and with my brother and in the mornings before school. They took everything to God because they wanted to make sure they made wise decisions, expressed their gratitude to God and knew what course to pursue.

Our family knew that everything was from God. Growing up with that kind of perspective really shapes your mind and your future.

Josh Price, Dale's son

⌘⌘⌘

I watched Ruby and Dale, how they followed God and loved each other - that was a good example.

They put God first in their lives. Regardless of the situation, from camp programs to cancer to Ruby's job changes, they always looked God and to the Bible for direction. That's how I want to be.

A big influence on me was the respect they had for each other. They went out of their way to lift the other person up, in what they did and what they said. Ruby would tell me, "Find the important ways to uplift your husband. Be positive with him and build him up, don't tear him down." I never ever saw them fight.

Amy, Matt's wife

⌘⌘⌘

I think a lot of people didn't think Ruby could cope with and manage what she was facing, those who thought she'd fall apart when the cancer battle went on for months, then years. I was sad for what she had to endure, but not worried she'd crumble or lose her faith in God. My mother-in-law is an incredibly strong woman. Strong in her love for her husband and in her relationship with God. She's very nurturing, always wanting to be with him. She loved reading to him, rubbing his feet, just being with him.

I also knew she wouldn't be alone. Her sons, Matt and Josh, love her in very supportive and timely ways. Their caring for her has helped allow her to continue living life, being involved with others – including our kids, their grandkids

> *Dad frequently shouted out, "Isn't God incredible!" always giving God credit for His handiwork and acknowledging Him as Almighty God. It wasn't an act or an attempt to show others how spiritual he was. That exclamation was just my dad's authentic response to what God had done and is doing.*

– even reaching out to grieve with others struggling with pain of their own.

Jennifer, Josh's wife

In some ways, my dad's cancer was a nightmare for my mom because of the retirement plans they had made together. But they comforted each other – as they'd always done – and made the most of the times they had. They changed diets together, exercised, read, just did everything they could together.

In Seattle, in between the appointments and treatments, they took people out to dinner, explored the city, and always found opportunities to share Christ with those who needed Him. Dad felt it was especially urgent to get the Gospel message out there whenever he could, so they weren't shy about sharing their story and the centrality of Christ to what they were experiencing.

She worked for the school district right up until her resignation in January 2011. It was hard for them to have her working while Dale was fighting cancer. She found it harder and harder to leave him for extended periods of time. He really needed her comfort but, at the same time, really wanted her to be able to continue her career in education.

Josh

ᐊᐁᐊ

Over the years, Dale has encouraged my growth in Christ more than any other person. He wrote a very special letter to us when we were getting ready to go to Malawi, Africa, for a short-term missions trip.

DEAR MATT and Amy,

It's a little hard for me to know what to write as you depart for Africa. None of us ever really know what the future holds. You will be on the other side of the world ministering to children who need the love of Christ to surround and embrace them. You will be the arms and hands of Jesus. On this side of the planet, I will be ministering the Gospel to children whose life experiences are very different, but whose need is just as great.

I know we will be connected by the same comforting Holy Spirit, but I will miss you. I have thought a great deal about what to say, knowing that I may not see you until you return.

First of all, I love you both. Not because of all the things you have done and will accomplish. I just love you with a father's love. You are precious to me and I am blessed to call you my children – my son and daughter. I will always love you.

Second, I am confident God will use you in mighty ways. He will change your lives forever. I am proud of your courage, your willingness to take this step of faith and your sacrifice of selfless obedience to God's leading.

Third, I will pray for you. I won't be able to hug you or call you and just say, "Hi!" But I pray that God will comfort you and give you His peace in ways I can't. I will also pray for your growth in Him, your strength in Him, and for your health and physical safety.

Last, I just want you both to know that this man has been blessed to be called your father. You both have changed my life.

I pray that we all would learn to live our lives in light of eternity. I have been reflecting on Colossians 3:1-4 this past week. "Therefore, if you have been raised up with Christ, keep seeking the things above, where Christ is, seated at the right hand of God. Set your minds on things above, not on the things that are on earth. For you have died and your life is hidden with Christ in God. When Christ, who is our life, is revealed, then you also shall be revealed with Him in glory."

I praise God for you both. I entrust your lives, ministry and return into His loving care.

All my love, Dad

> *Dale wrote this letter to Matt and me, but I believe it is his heart for every one of us. The passion he had for the Gospel, for people and for the Lord is something that I hope to pass on to my children.*

ை்ை்ை்

The CaringBridge Connection

Editor's Note: *The first paragraph is Dale's greeting to everyone as they signed on to CaringBridge. The second paragraph is what Dale had to say about CaingBridge. The rest are just a smattering of the thousands of loving tributes to the Prices.*

THIS IS the story of our journey with the Great Shepherd into the valley of the shadow of death. This online resource helps connect us with you. We're grateful for CaringBridge.

I AM glad we have CaringBridge as a way to keep in touch. One reason I like it is because I can get a glimpse of what people are thinking about me. It's kind of like attending your own funeral and hearing everything – without actually having to die!

Dale, I have enjoyed your journal entries and always come away lifted up and encouraged. You are making the most of each day, as we all should. For us to let a single day pass without praising and thanking God, is real negligence on our parts.

I am very glad that you had the opportunity in Russia, that the trip went smoothly and safely, and that you now are sharing your adventure with so many. God is using you, and you are a very willing servant. I pray that you are comfortable this evening. I look forward to seeing you again.

My heart is full, knowing that God is being honored with every breath you take and that He is answering our prayers to heal you. I am also touched and inspired by your humility and desire to live your moments in high definition. It is a sweet spot, to be in the palm of God's hands as He moves and directs our lives.

ᴈᴈᴈ

Dear Dale (or, as we know you better, Buzz!) - We are praising the Lord for you and your family! Our God is an awesome God and we are thankful to Him for seeing fit to give you "exceedingly, abundantly above all that we ask or think." Praise the Lord for your healing; praise the Lord for your ministry; and praise the Lord for your testimony and faith!

ᴈᴈᴈ

It has been so encouraging to read your entries. Life is indeed a mix of the good the bad and the ugly. I continue to pray for your good health and remission status.

ᴈᴈᴈ

You both are in my heart, thoughts and prayers today. Thank you for being the amazing man and woman of God you are. You are both such wonderful examples to me, and I cannot even begin to describe how much of a blessing you both have been throughout my entire life.

I wouldn't love Jesus as much as I do today if it weren't for your constant faith, love, support and daily example of Christ likeness! Thank you for your love for Jesus, your marriage and love for each other - and your love for all of God's people.

ᴈᴈᴈ

I know radiation treatments can be rough on the brain and make one very fatigued, so I pray for your physical strength, Dale. Oh, how I love you so much and am so thankful for all you've taught (and continue to teach) me.

You are a walking example of how a Christian should live and act on this earth. What an example you are to all of us. This is a very difficult and, I am sure, confusing time for you and Ruby. God has a plan, though, so trust and continue to abide in him.

⊰⊱⊰⊱

You two have touched thousands and thousands of lives for Christ in so many ways. Canyonview Camp has had a huge impact on so many children over the years, too. All that to say, I prayed earnestly for you two today! Blessings on you as you continue your walk.

⊰⊱⊰⊱

Dale and Ruby, I don't know if you remember me or not. We met at the UW Hospital, in the radiation lobby. (My husband was having radiation the same time you were.) Ruby gave me a copy of a sermon you had given, Dale. I think about you often and will continue to keep you and your family in my prayers. May God continue to bless you with His love.

⊰⊱⊰⊱

Even as busy as your lives always have been, Dale and Ruby, you always seem to have time to listen, and you always seem to take an interest in the welfare of others. That is such a rare quality in our busy and self-focused world. The wide reach of your love for others is clearly reflected in the huge outpouring of love you have received during your struggle with this cancer.

⊰⊱⊰⊱

Ruby, something you said during my time at Canyonview has always stuck with me. You asked me if I found that Jesus Christ was enough. If you remember, I was so sick for so long (and still am), but my answer was and still is, Yes! Jesus Christ is enough, more than enough.

෧෧෧

Thank you so much for your willingness to write about His help and grace and love that is bringing you and your wife and family through victoriously. Thank you for being His mouthpiece, His instrument of encouragement and displaying His love so powerfully. Regardless of the time you have on this earth, I know you will finish victoriously and by His grace (1 Corinthians 9:24-27).

I will continue to lift you and all your family up in prayer as this is the most powerful thing we can do right now. I sure love you so much and although I am saddened by the recent developments, I know it is all part of the master plan for your life. Thank you for sharing your journey with us.

෧෧෧

You and Ruby are the true meaning of "love" and I only hope to be like you both. I got tears in my eyes as you talked about your battle with cancer, because that is what it is, a battle, and you are fighting hard.

෧෧෧

Sometimes we leave things unsaid that should have been said long ago, so today I'm urged in my spirit to tell you what your influence has meant to me.

I have often said that you were like a second father to me. You taught me to be a student of God's Word. You cared about me and asked how I was doing and truly listened. You saw leadership potential in me and called it out.

৯৯৯

God, in His infinite wisdom and great mercy, is demonstrating to me through you and your testimony how to walk in the wilderness; how to suffer for His name's sake; how to rejoice in the midst of a trial; and how to "let everything that hath breath praise the LORD."

৯৯৯

Here's what stands out to me when I think about how you are handling your cancer: Your courage, faith and hope. You have not given up!

I'm amazed at how you keep pressing on, more for the love of your family than for yourself. Many lesser men, me included, would probably have given in, lain down and died by now. But not Dale.

At the same time, Ruby's strength is incredible. People in my own family have had cancer, so I know from experience how hard it is to simply get through the day, let alone remain positive and be able to give to others. She is doing an amazing job, supporting your decisions and focusing on one day at a time. I know she is extremely heartbroken over all that has happened, but she does her best every day. I admire her fortitude so much!

STEP BY STEP

November 15, 2009

Ruby and I got home to Creswell on Wednesday night and turned around Thursday morning so Ruby could attend a conference in Portland. While she does that, I am sitting on a Saturday morning in a coffee shop along the Willamette River, looking at the river and the beauty of the changing seasons.

Our next chemo treatment will be our first one in Eugene. It will be nice to lose the 12-hour trip to and from Seattle. We'll return to Seattle after Christmas for a CAT scan and a new MRI of my brain.

We praise God and rejoice, knowing that your prayers and ours have combined before our God as He allows us to continue in His service on this planet for a while more. Thank you for your faithfulness in remembering us. We feel surrounded by love and kindness.

December 16, 2009

Merry Christmas! I realize that this a Christmas we thought I might never see. The journey over the past 16 months has been torturous at times, but it has never been lonely! We have been encouraged, loved, prayed for and ministered to in countless ways all along this path God has laid before us.

Sometimes, as I have lain awake at night, I have prayed for an even greater awareness of God's abiding presence. I want the emotion His presence brings, not just the confident knowledge.

I continue to be mostly pain-free and all my body parts, including my mind, seem to be working. I had chemo last week in Eugene, but I've had more nausea since then. My next appointment will be in Seattle later this month and will include a CAT scan, an MRI, and chemotherapy. We pray that Seattle's anti-nausea regimen will work better than the one used in Eugene.

December 31, 2009

Happy New Year! Praise God for His mercy and grace!

One year ago we had no idea what 2009 would bring. Among the things we didn't know were coming as we ended 2008:

- Opportunities with the Christian-camping ministry in Russia
- Lost functionality in my left arm and leg in April

- The cancer metastasized to my brain and then to my back.
- The targeted cancer drug, Tarceva, produced severe nausea and weight loss (without providing a positive effect on my cancer).
- The whole-brain radiation and gamma-knife procedures – along with your prayers – restored my left-side functionality completely.
- Doors for ministry opened in Creswell, as Ruby became school superintendent.
- Ruby's father and my dad both went home to be with the Lord.
- God's provision of many speaking opportunities and divine appointments.
- The Christian Camp and Conference Association conference in Colorado Springs was a greater blessing than we could have imagined

These challenges and blessings have poured out all along this walk of faith. It is an amazing blessing to see God's perfect will unfold day after day.

A few days ago Ruby and I were in Seattle for tests and treatments. It started with a CAT scan and a blood-draw (for my pre-chemo analysis). At 10 a.m. we met with Dr. Martins, who gave an encouraging report.

My blood work looks good and the CAT scan showed no cancer activity in my right lung. Then it was off to the lab for an H1N1 (swine flu) shot, followed by my chemo. Three hours later we headed to the University District for a bite of lunch, and then to the University of Washington hospital for my MRI.

Tuesday started much easier. Our only appointment was with Dr. Patel, to review my MRI. The news was all good. The five tumor sites in my brain don't appear to be active at this time and all have decreased in size. The two small cancer sites identified last summer are no longer identifiable. Then, after picking up a couple of prescriptions and scheduling our next visits, we were on our way to Oregon and our family.

February 2, 2010

I have neglected my journal for four weeks. There is much to catch you up on.

Since my last journal entry I have gone through another round of chemo, tolerating the treatment well and having very little nausea.

Thank you for your prayers. My next treatment will be the week after I return from Russia.

I seem to be enjoying a place of still waters and pleasant pastures, to use a metaphor from Psalm 23. Since I wrote last I have had no physical changes — no pain or other symptoms. Praise God! I don't believe the cancer is gone, but my immediate home-going doesn't seem to be in sight.

March 8, 2010

On the 21st of February Ruby and I celebrated our 40th wedding anniversary. It was a beautiful day surrounded by friends and family. We exchanged vows. I have never felt more blessed in our 40 years of marriage than I did on that day. I was honored to express to her my vows of faithfulness and love. Her words to me were filled with devotion, faith and hope. I will never forget the light of love shining in her eyes.

Last week we attended a Christian Camp and Conference Association regional conference at Cannon Beach Conference Center in Oregon. It was a blessed time, especially because Ruby was able to be there for the first half of the meetings.

God knew what we needed to hear, as always, so it shouldn't have been a surprise that our speaker shared from the first few chapters of 2 Corinthians. Chapter 1 reminds us that God is the one who comforts us when we suffer affliction. But that's not all. He also, simultaneously, gives us the privilege of comforting others with the comfort we've received from God. Many of you have been the fulfillment of this passage in my life - you have been agents of God's comfort.

March 16, 2010

One of the hardest things for me has been realizing I'm not in control. I'm finding out what it means to really and completely give over control of my life (and the lives of those I love) to God. It's not my natural response when facing tough situations and it's not easy.

The reward, however, is well worth the effort. The Lord provides such a sweetness when I'm wholly dependent on Him and there is great power in trusting Him with that which I cannot control.

Recently, I have had increased pain in my lower back and my hips. The pain is like a bad memory from last summer, when we found that the cancer had metastasized to my sacrum and left hip. There may be other reasons for the pain - like going snowboarding two weeks ago with Ruby, our son Josh, and grandsons Tyler and Cody. It was amazing to have three generations flying down Mt. Bachelor!

But here's the bottom line: apart from Extra-Strength Tylenol, the pain will not go away. When I got my chemo treatment last week I told my oncologist about the pain, and he ordered the MRI on my low back and hips. Today we meet with him and get the test results.

March 25, 2010

We met with my medical oncologist from Willamette Valley Cancer Institute after an MRI on my lower back and hips nearly two weeks ago. He gave us the difficult news that the cancer in my sacrum and adjoining iliac bones is active and growing slowly. He scheduled a next-day meeting for us with my radiation oncologist.

That evening was difficult for us. It seemed impossible to not contemplate the future. We had, of course, been hoping that the cancer would continue its retreat, but the Lord had a different path for us on our journey.

The following day we met with our radiation oncologist. He was encouraging about the potential effectiveness of a course of radiation treatment. He recommended that we begin a round of 15 days of radiation on early April, shortly after meeting with the team at Seattle Cancer Care Alliance.

April 12, 2010

Thanks for your prayers. We have been busy living, loving, serving and getting medical checks. After I spoke at the sunrise service at Canyonview on Easter morning, we threw our suitcases in the car, went to the Easter service in Silverton, and then drove to Seattle.

Our meetings with our doctors to go over the results of my lab tests, brain-MRI, lung CAT scan, and meet with my radiation oncologist were very encouraging. It appears that there is no recent cancer activity in my brain or lung. My medical oncologist was not convinced the cancer was advancing in my sacrum and wanted to schedule three more rounds of chemo before deciding whether or not to begin radiation on my back. I got chemo on Tuesday afternoon.

I'll have a biopsy done on my lower back to see if the cancerous tissue matches the specific requirements of a new study. If it does, I may qualify to participate in a new drug trial. The first round of this trial has been very positive and we're hoping my cancer matches.

We are always so thankful for the loving care given us at Seattle Cancer Care and also Willamette Cancer Center.

April 26, 2010

My life, as always is in His hands. Whom or what shall I fear?

I want you to know what my thoughts have centered on recently. This passage, Psalm 63:3-8, may help you know how God has been teaching and sustaining me lately:

"BECAUSE THY LOVINGKINDNESS IS BETTER THAN LIFE,
MY LIPS WILL PRAISE THEE.
SO I WILL BLESS THEE AS LONG AS I LIVE:
I WILL LIFT UP MY HANDS IN THY NAME.
MY SOUL IS SATISFIED AS WITH MARROW AND FATNESS,
AND MY MOUTH OFFERS PRAISE WITH JOYFUL LIPS.
WHEN I REMEMBER THEE ON MY BED,
I MEDITATE ON THEE IN THE NIGHT WATCHES,
FOR THOU HAST BEEN MY HELP.
AND IN THE SHADOW OF THY WINGS I SING FOR JOY.
MY SOUL CLINGS TO THEE; THY RIGHT HAND UPHOLDS ME."

Tomorrow I get chemo, this time in Eugene. Three weeks later I will get chemo in Seattle, along with an MRI or CAT scan of my lower back. We're also awaiting the results of the biopsy from my lower back and hoping to find out if I qualify for a new targeted drug trial.

The pain in my back has worsened, but I'm not sure if that is due to the cancer or because of my increased exercise. Regardless, my health and all these medical procedures are part of my life now. I am thankful for the caring doctors and nurses around us, but I continue

"The Lord provides such a sweetness when I'm wholly dependent on Him and there is great power in trusting Him with that which I cannot control."

to entrust my life to the Great Physician who loves me, and knows my name.

May 14, 2010

Lately, my doctors have been giving me information and guidance that I don't like very much.

"Don't snowboard anymore; the risk of serious injury is greatly increased now that your bones have been weakened by chemo and radiation treatments."

"You've lost about 30 percent of your right lung's capacity, so avoid strenuous physical activity or you will be winded."

These developments are unpleasant but hardly shocking. Whether it's because of age, illness or a disease like cancer, we all face declining physical or mental capabilities sooner or later. And we don't like that!

When I received chemo two weeks ago my doctors and I decided to include some bone-strengthening therapy with the anti-cancer drugs. That approach sounded great, but two days later my knees began to swell (a side effect that had been mentioned) and any leg movements produced great pain. Pain killers, ice, heat and elevating my legs didn't seem to help much. While we were in Port Orford last weekend for one of Matt's music concerts, we drove to our favorite beach with Matt, Amy, Noah, and Logan. Unfortunately the pain in my knees made playing - and even walking down to the beach with my family - impossible.

After church this Sunday, Ruby and I head back to Seattle. I'll have MRIs on my brain and back, and my next round of chemo on Monday and Tuesday. The biopsy conducted five weeks ago was inconclusive since there was no cancer cells found at the site where the samples were taken. We'll be discussing the possibility of another biopsy when we meet with the oncologists.

God already knows the answers. We're just walking by faith as His path unfolds before us.

Love, Dale

Chapter 6

You Changed My Life

"My days, weeks, months or possibly even years are in His hands. He knows my prognosis and He wrote it before I was born. The question is, do I trust His plan? He has made it plain that He still has work for me to do and His perfect plan will be accomplished by an imperfect cancer patient, me. My cancer has prepared me to do this work like nothing ever has. It is, for me, the Refiner's fire."

It's impossible to adequately tell the complete story of Dale and Ruby's influence on others, but that's no reason not to try!

In this chapter, people describe what the Prices meant to them. Lives changed, marriages saved, relationships begun and nurtured, hurts healed, ministries launched...the list of the ways they blessed others truly goes on and on. Heading that list, of course, is Dale and Ruby's spiritual impact on people – helping kids, adults, and youth find and follow Jesus Christ.

Dale is the focus of most of the comments you'll read, but he wasn't on his own; Ruby was right there every step of the way. Dale would be the first to say that much of what people gained from him was due to his wife and the ways God used her to shape his life.

Dale often described himself as a healthy man...who happened to have cancer. A child of God, he explained, is defined by his relationship with God and people, not by a diagnosis or an illness. Dale and Ruby always valued people and their importance to God above any program, ministry, appointment, or activity.

Over the 32 months of Dale's cancer battle, hundreds of friends, family members, professional colleagues and ministry partners had opportunities to express how much they were blessed by the Prices' presence in their lives – and in the lives of countless others.

First impressions are lasting impressions

The first time Dale met with the local pastors in our community, his heart for the Lord and for ministry simply won us over. Dale became our friend, our colleague and our brother in Christ. He preached several times at my church and at least once in every church in town. The beat of Dale's heart was for the greater good of the church, regardless of the name on the door. He also spent a good deal of one-on-one time with me and the other pastors, sharing our journeys of faith.

ക∙ക∙ക

When I first got to know Dale Price I discovered that he was one the most brilliant and godly teachers I'd ever met. At that time he was the interim pastor at our church and was especially great with children. He did wonderful sermons for the kids, gathering them in close to him, right in the front of the sanctuary.

Shortly after my sons and I started attending the Baptist church in Silverton, Dale greeted me and asked how I was. "Awful," I said. At the time I was recently divorced, didn't know anyone and felt very alone. But he introduced me to Ruby, and she and I began a lifelong friendship. The Prices and my family did a lot together, especially skiing, water sports, and other outdoor activities.

Dale and Ruby came alongside us at the right times and in the right ways. When my oldest son was killed in car accident, he and Ruby walked through the pain and loss with me. Another time, when a house fire destroyed our house and nearly everything in it, they helped me get back on my feet.

In the 29 years I've known Dale I can't remember one negative interaction with him. Even when he was displeased with something, he was kind and respectful when he expressed himself.

ക∙ക∙ക

Ruby and Dale, I thank the Lord for giving you to me early in my life. It was so wonderful to hear

Dale tell me that Jesus Christ was offering me free salvation! There was nothing I could do to earn it. If it were not for your diligence to teach me God's Word clearly and lovingly, I wouldn't be strong in my walk with the Lord.

⮞⮞⮞

Ruby, I don't know if you remember me (I was in a women's Bible study you led while I was in college), but I have thought of you often over the years. You had a huge influence on the development of my Christian walk, first as a young woman, and then as a new wife. Your life and teaching pointed the way for a Christian woman to live with Jesus at the center of everything.

Your love for Jesus and your love for Dale were like shining lights to me as I navigated through the early years of my marriage. God used you and Dale to point me in the right direction, and I am grateful for the love you poured into my life.

Special relationships

I will always consider myself blessed because of your unconditional love and commitment to me. Your influence on my life has impacted additional generations - my children years ago and, now, my grandchildren. I followed your example and have spent hours mentoring and discipling young people. Just like I was, these kids I work with struggle and need someone to believe in them, love them, and point them to our Father in heaven.

Ruby, I know your journey has not been easy and it's not what you ever planned or dreamed of for this time of your life. But, amazingly, you have been faithful in your service to God, Dale, your children, your students, me and so many others. As the Scripture says, "They will rise up and call you blessed."

Thank you for always seeing me with the eyes of faith, encouraging me to become a woman of God. You modeled Christlikeness so I knew what it was and could see it lived out. As a result, you are the woman I want to be like. I pray that God will use me to minister to you and allow me to give back what was so generously given to me.

⁊⁊⁊

I wasn't the only person in my family to have a wonderful relationship with Dale. When my daughter was 9 and in love with horses, my wife and I thought of Dale and Canyonview. We signed her up as a camper because we knew the quality of Dale and his organization.

Today, partly through Dale's mentoring, my daughter has gone on to missions work in Africa, assisting AIDS orphans and the poor. Three years ago she started a volunteer-run weekly meal for the homeless in Carlsbad, Calif., called Fill-a-Belly. This organization has provided thousands of meals and countless hours of Christian fellowship for those they call "travelers."

Dale's connection to just one of his campers, my daughter in this case, has led to hundreds, maybe thousands of personal connections on two continents. Now multiply that by the number of people he touched at Canyonview Camp, the churches where he and Ruby served, the entire communities they touched – not to mention those affected by his cancer – and you begin to understand the scope of Dale's influence.

❧❧❧

Dale would not only ask me how things were going, he really wanted to know the answer to his question. That's not often the case with most people. Our conversations nearly always focused on the Lord and His impact in my life, as well as in the lives of others.

Once, when I was broken and falling apart, I called Dale. He dropped everything and came to our house where we prayed, looked at truths from the Bible, and talked about what I should do, and where my focus should be. He wanted me to have a healthy marriage, encouraging me and my husband to love each other deeply, making sure God was the center of our family.

❧❧❧

Dale had a serving heart, as well as strong leadership and teaching gifts. People fell in love with Canyonview because of his love for kids and the ways he trained them up in the Lord. He really was one of a kind and had relationships with people that were personal and unique, too. Dale loved everyone, never dodged people's questions and made you feel like you were the most important person in his world.

❧❧❧

Ruby and I have known each other for a long time. We'd often sit and talk, blessed by the multiple ways God would speak to and through us. Sometimes, the experience of encountering the Lord with one another and sensing His presence brought us to tears.

❧❧❧

Dale was always interested in my family and stayed involved in our kids' lives over the years. Our daughters were at Canyonview, both as campers and as staff. When our son had cancer as a child, we knew some people would pull away because they didn't know what to do or say. But we also knew Dale and Ruby would hang in there with us, which they did.

I'm thankful for the times Dale and I had later in life, when our kids were grown and we had more opportunities to meet man to man, ministering equally to each other. I appreciated the many times when he ministered to me and to my marriage over the years, but the mutual ministry to one another was especially gratifying to me.

Courage. If you're looking a one-word description of Dale, that's the one. He didn't just accept and surrender to the bad things he encountered, but met them head-on, refusing to give up. That mentality allowed him to continue his ministry to thousands, even as his earthly life was coming to a close. He ministered to others who also had challenging, even terminal, situations, as well as those who were caring for him.

Today, Dale would probably say "If I only could do more..." or "If I could just pass the Word of God onto one more person...." Dale's message and teachings, however, are without limits. His message is being spread throughout the world through the lives of those he's influenced.

I'll never forget the time

My big brother Dale was always very thoughtful and caring. Once, when I was only 3 or 4, we went to get a Popsicle. He had to take me home because I became frightened by some noisy construction equipment. I was very sad, knowing I wasn't going to get a Popsicle. I was wrong, though. My hero, Dale, soon returned with Popsicles for both of us!

Another time our family was at the beach. Dale made me breakfast and then took me by the hand as we walked on the beach and he taught me about life in the tide pools.

In school I wrote him a short letter. It was from my heart but contained many misspellings, including the word "brother." Over the years, "my bather" became a phrase Dale cherished. He kept that letter for more than 50 years and returned it to me just two weeks before he died.

My Bather Dale

My bather Dale and me are good bathers.

We do laes to things.

Here are some of the things that we do.

We go wakeing all over the bech and we go rowing in the rowboat.

We do laes of ather things.

Dale committed his life to Christ just after I had accepted Jesus as my Savior. I had received very little spiritual guidance until I had the opportunity to drive with him across the U.S. For more than a week I had him all to myself (a rarity). That road trip became a one-week discipleship course as I barraged him with questions about being a Christian.

It was at this time that he also brought Ruby into my life. Her commitment to Christ was also radiant and she experienced the additional deluge of questions from me about our faith. What a blessing those two have been!

ఞ×ఞ×ఞ

It was 2 a.m., I was alone and stranded in a sea of emotional and spiritual darkness, when I cried out to God and asked for help. He whispered, "Call Dale Price."

With wrenching tears and a desperate heart, I picked up the phone and asked for Dale's help. He and Ruby had little kids at home, but he didn't hesitate to jump in his truck and come rescue me.

He moved me and my belongings into his home, where I lived for about a year. During that time Dale taught me the Word and he and Ruby opened their lives to me on the deepest and most-vulnerable levels. They took a risk on a little waif with a history of anger, bitterness and destructive behavior that must have rivaled that of any teenager they knew at the time.

He gave me a job at the camp and then helped me enroll in Bible college. After I moved into housing at the camp I slowly began to learn how to be a

Deep Dale, I used to call it, when he'd get very serious about whatever the topic was. That's when I found out just how passionate he was about submitting his will to God's will and what a skilled and effective Bible teacher he was.

friend to others; how to love and give; and how to grow – first, in Christ, then as a person.

Dale taught me so much and encouraged me along the way. He taught me to sing and worship; how to have real fun and laugh; and how to work for something meaningful and valuable.

I am 50 years old now and continue to walk with God. He is my best friend, mostly because I learned about Him first in the faces of Dale and Ruby Price. Through the way they love others, the Lord has revealed Himself countless times to the thousands who've been touched by the Prices.

Dale was an active and much-loved part of the community. In addition to his church-leadership and camp-director roles, Dale spoke to countless school and civic groups, and served 30 years with the Kiwanis Club. A highlight of the local Oktoberfest event each autumn was Dale's promotion of the virtues and deliciousness of German sausages. You could hear his voice booming across the grounds as he let loose with his famous sales pitch:

> *A loaf of bread!*
> *A pound of meat!!*
> *And all the mustard you can eat!!!*

I had known Ruby from school and through Pooh's Corner when our kids were young, but didn't really know Dale that well. It was years later that our Kiwaniannes group joined the Kiwanis, and we began working on many projects and attending meetings together every Thursday morning at 7 a.m.

*Dale had routinely visited the Kiwaniannes'
meetings so he was someone we all knew and
trusted. Dale made us feel comfortable with
the merge. More importantly, he made us all
feel important and needed. He sat amongst
the ladies and was purposeful in drawing us
into the conversation, always taking time to be
complimentary of someone's actions whenever
possible. He was a wizard at diplomacy; he
was so honest and truly meant whatever he did
or said. Dale always made the meetings fun,
and if for some reason a speaker didn't show
up, he could pull something out of his hat and
keep us interested for the next half hour.*

*We were all devastated when we heard of
Dale's cancer and mentioned him at most every
meeting during his treatments. Many times
when discussing a project or program, you
would hear "Well, when Dale did that......" He
made a lasting impression on all of us!*

*For me personally, Dale was a great friend and
someone I admired and respected. Dale always
had good sound advice for me regarding city
politics, and he could make me laugh at myself
and feel like any challenge could be resolved.*

*Dale led by example and his example was
good, kind and caring. I will always treasure
our friendship and miss his infectious laugh, wit
and twinkle in his eye.*

৶৶৶

God gave Dale opportunities to share Christ because of his
cancer, opportunities he never would have had otherwise. And,
he hated when he had to turn down a chance to serve God
by serving others. God gave him the spiritual, emotional and

physical strength to keep up his hectic schedule of teaching, conferences, leading the camp and even going to Russia.

Dale took on even more humility as the cancer progressed. More than once he wrote in his journal the promise of 2 Corinthians 9:10: "MY GRACE IS SUFFICIENT FOR YOU, FOR MY STRENGTH IS MADE PERFECT IN WEAKNESS." Because of his cancer, Dale had additional opportunities for God's strength to work through his weakness.

Dale was - Jesus with skin on

You have given me and thousands of others an example of what it truly means to follow in Christ's steps. Dale, you've been tireless, faithful, and loving in your commitments to the people God has entrusted to your care. You've been a spiritual father to me, and I am committed to live out your legacy by imitating you as you have imitated Christ. Your toil and labor was not in vain.

Dale, you were a spiritual father to me, and one of the reasons I am serving God today. Thank you for believing in me when I didn't believe in myself and for seeing things in me I didn't. I pray that I can pass on to others the gift you gave to me.

The thread that's been woven through my life is the Prices' faith in God and how they modeled that faith to the world. Their marriage, how they treated me and their character drew me to them. They were the warmest, most nurturing, positive and growth-producing people I'd ever been around.

They didn't have a fairy-tale life, but I knew it was real and it was because of God. I knew I wanted what they had. Like it says in Hebrews, "...remember those who led you...imitate their faith." Imitating Dale and Ruby's faith – that's what inspires me.

I appreciate them because although they couldn't take me out of my circumstances, they could point me toward God and his Word. What they stood for and taught me really increased my faith.

❧❧❧

Beyond all of Dale's accomplishments in life, his resilient faith is what characterized his life. He exemplified the man spoken of by King David in the first Psalm. Dale's life was richly blessed because he did not pattern his life according to the counsel of wicked men, nor did he sit amongst those who scoff at every good thing in life. His delight, of course, was in God's Word, upon which he meditated both day and night.

As a result, Dale became like a tree that was planted near a river that flowed with abundant water. His roots went deep and he was able to bear abundant spiritual fruit both in his life and in the lives of others. Such fruit was born not just when it was most likely, but also when it was most unlikely. Indeed, Dale prospered in all that he did, and his life bore clear and unmistakable testimony to that effect.

❧❧❧

Ephesians 4:12 says, "IT WAS HE WHO GAVE SOME TO BE PASTORS AND TEACHERS TO PREPARE GOD'S PEOPLE FOR WORKS OF SERVICE SO THAT THE BODY OF CHRIST MAY BE BUILT UP." *I had the privilege, as many of you, of working and serving with Dale at Canyonview Camp. I served in Day Camp, Overnight Camps, the Canadian Bike trip (at first ONLY because a GIRL had signed up so I HAD to go). We were always involved in various construction, maintenance projects along with memorably putting screws in the Equestrian Center Roof. Years later Dale brought to my attention – we put 20,000 screws in the roof!*

He mentored as he taught and trusted me. Dale didn't micro manage. I learned by watching and doing. God's word was taught and lived out daily. He began each day with us in prayer and in God's word. We ended each day with thankfulness for God's provision whether it was around the campfire or the flagpole or under the stars on Vancouver Island. I was a counselor under his leadership, beside him as an assistant director in Day Camp and on bike trips and then co-directed instead of him. There was nothing we didn't do, from cleaning outhouses to treating the lake. There was joy in serving.

Dale's love for God's word, teaching us to share it, enables me today to have confidence in the power of God through His word. "...How loving and patient He must be, cause He's still workin' on me."

❧❧❧

Dale honored me with a personal phone call to tell me of the diagnosis. It was hard to believe that a lifelong non-smoker could have the dread disease associated with the use of tobacco, or that my brother in the Lord of the same age was facing his mortality. From the outset,

Dale's outlook was mature, his expectations realistic, his courage palpable, his determination inspiring, and his hope contagious. I was one of the elders who anointed Dale with oil and prayed for his healing on the basis of evidence that his conscience was clear before God and man. All of us were humbled by the grace and goodness of God as our identification with each other cast us tearfully but joyfully on His mercy.

Early on, Dale described himself as a healthy man who happened to have cancer. A child of God is defined by his relationship with God, not by an illness. His relationships with Ruby, his family, and grandsons have been a constant source of comfort and motivation. Dale began to talk about life in Hi-Def, focusing on the ministries God kept adding to his to-do list. He once described his situation as a man whose boat capsized in shark-infested waters and whose choice was to discharge his responsibility by swimming for shore. As he continued to swim, it was not without dependence on the support of Ruby, his family, church family, Canyonview team, and many people praying. His faithfulness in communicating through CaringBridge and Jaira Hill magnified a testimony gone viral, comforting those who are in any affliction with the same comfort with which he and Ruby are comforted by God (2 Corinthians 1:3-4).

Ruby's devotion to Dale is obvious – not only as a dutiful wife, but as one who shared his passion to manifest the fragrance of Christ in reactions to good and bad news, as well as in actions to redeem the time. I have been most impressed by her honesty, transparency and vulnerability as she waited on the Lord with Dale. It's not about our trust that never wavers, but about our sometimes wavering faith in Jesus who never fails.

Shortly before Dale passed away, he and I spent three hours together in his living room. That day, Dale and I were blessed by God. During those three hours, Dale touched God's glory and it touched him. Those moments of the Lord's glory illuminated our need to set aside personal agendas and plans, so we could be purified by the true spirituality from above.

One other aspect of Dale that everyone was aware of but few actually grasped was Colonel Dale Price, who at the time of his retirement after 30 years of service to our country, was the State Emergency Preparedness Liaison Officer to the State of Oregon. Dale taught a Sunday School class for years, yet once a month, he'd have to find a substitute because he would be off doing his military duty. Occasionally he would pop into the church building with his camos on - meeting, greeting, teaching, ministering to, serving others.

Throughout his three-year command, Colonel Price placed special emphasis on the Family Support Program, initiated training programs designed to allow soldiers to grow and excel which manifested itself in a 100 percent retention program throughout his command, and labeled Colonel Price as the best battalion commander in the 4th Brigade.

As the Oregon State Emergency Preparedness Liaison Officer from 21 July 1994 to 7 July 1999, Colonel Price's sterling performance during the Oregon Floods of February 1996 assured rapid response to critical demands in a time-

sensitive and highly visible setting. Colonel Price unselfishly provided volunteer hours in the Joint Operations Coordination Center for the NIKE World Masters Games, August 1998. His input at numerous exercises and conferences facilitated the establishment of comprehensive plans and policies for future emergency response efforts.

Earning the coveted Ranger Tab early in his career, Colonel Price represents the embodiment of pride and professionalism. Outstanding leadership, unique professional capabilities, devotion to duty, and significant achievements during this period and throughout his career in the United States Army are in keeping with the highest traditions of military service and reflect great credit to himself, Fifth United States Army and the United States Army Reserve.

The CaringBridge connection

You are a light in this dark world, shining brightly as you have been from the beginning. You are like a lighthouse, guiding the ships along the shore in the roughest of storms. We love you, Dale.

ఞఞఞ

Dale and Ruby - Our conversation at the Portland airport this past Thursday has put you and your family in my thoughts, in my heart, and in my prayers.

I was deeply touched and inspired by your faithful witness and positive attitude. I was also moved by your capacity to think of others before yourselves. Even in the midst of your most-recent challenges, and before sharing any personal news, you inquired about our daughter, Erica, who had been in a severe car accident almost two years ago.

Hearing you talk, seeing your smile (truly, a window to the heart!), sharing your journey of enduring faith and love of God, has blessed and humbled me more than words can say.

శళళ

Ruby's devotion to Dale is obvious – not only as a dutiful wife, but as one who shared his passion to manifest the fragrance of Christ in reactions to good and bad news, as well as in actions to redeem the time.

The Dove of Forgiveness, inspired by Jennifer

STEP BY STEP

June 11, 2010

I've really been out of touch for the past few weeks, the result of a busy life with cancer and ministry. And there has been a little too much pain when I sit down at the computer. But there have been wonderful times at the feet of Jesus, with our family, and with our brothers and sisters in Silverton, Creswell, and at Canyonview.

I'll give you some of the sequence on my cancer treatments over the last couple of months. After my trip to Seattle in the early April, the test results indicated that there were no cancer cells in the biopsy sample. The doctor called with the news two weeks later, saying, "Don't rejoice yet. The lack of cancer probably just means they missed the site by as little as half an inch."

We traveled back to Seattle in May for another MRI and PET scan which showed that the cancer is active in my hips which also confirmed that further chemo was not profitable. I was then scheduled for another biopsy on my back. I got it on June 4.

While we are waiting for results on the biopsy we got the OK from the Seattle oncologists to pursue radiation treatments on my back at the earliest possible date. We could do this now because the PET scan did show a small nodule of cancer growing on my right lung. That nodule will be the next site for a biopsy if the one from my back is negative.

Ruby and I met with our medical and radiation oncologists here in Eugene yesterday and today, and started the first of 16 radiation treatments on my lower back today. While we get the radiation treatments, we wait in hope.

August 12, 2010

We traveled to Seattle on August 1 and returned home a week later. The time away was a bit of a rollercoaster emotionally.

We began the week with both an MRI and a CAT scan. The news we received from those tests was not what we had hoped; the CAT scan showed cancer activity in both my right and left lungs (in the past, only the right lung had been infected). My oncologist described the cancer as being "out of control." We also found out that I didn't qualify for the drug trial we had hoped for.

We praise God, however, because the MRI showed no cancer activity in my brain, and my back seems to be responding well to the treatment.

The news from the MRI and CAT scan meant we had to adjust our plan of attack and determine the most effective course of treatment for the immediate future. Chemo appears to be the best option, since it is a systemic (whole-body) treatment. Dr. Martins said chemo was the treatment most likely to bring the cancer back under control.

In three weeks we'll hit the two-year anniversary of the cancer diagnosis. Living with cancer has been an amazing experience. These two years have been filled with hope, fear, love, thanksgiving, kindness, love and mercy. I have learned to see life with high-definition eyes and recognize that every day abounds with divinely-appointed ministry opportunities.

Let me describe some of what I have learned in the past two years:

1.   Cancer is the method God is using to put the final changes on my life. Holiness is not yet complete and He loves me enough to commit His attention to my perfection. Learning to be patient and listen to the gentle voice of the Spirit is hard work. I need to be quiet as I learn at the Savior's feet. It is so easy to want to interrupt and tell him how He ought to be doing this project called "me." So I wait, knowing that He who began His good work in me will complete it and I will be like Jesus.

2.   My days, weeks, months or possibly even years are in His hands. He knows my prognosis and He wrote it before I was born. The question is, do I trust His plan? He has made it plain that He still has work for me to do and His perfect plan will be accomplished by an imperfect cancer patient, me. My cancer has prepared me to do this work like nothing ever has. It is, for me, the Refiner's fire.

3.   He has provided me with His perfect armor. I have put on the armor again as the battle comes to me once again. Although my physical strength is fading I dwell securely in His strength. His sword (the Word) is the only weapon I need. The Evil One cannot hurt me.

September 5, 2010

It is hard to believe that my last journal entry was three weeks ago! Some events happened yesterday that moved me to write today. I just couldn't wait.

Yesterday, while munching down my granola, banana, and soy milk, I was reading from Chapter 6 of 2 Corinthians. The Apostle Paul reminds us that "now" is the "day of salvation," and to live accordingly. In verses 3 and 4 he tells us to never to give a cause for offense in anything and to commend ourselves in everything, in order to never discredit the ministry God has given us.

That morning I didn't know that my faith – and the ministry God has given me - would be greatly tested before midnight.

After lying down to take a nap early that afternoon, I woke up a few minutes later gasping for breath and frightened. After this happened several more times, I gave up on the nap and walked around outside, trying to breathe deeply. Sitting upright helped and although I longed for that nap I feared the feeling of suffocation more.

Ruby was at a welcome-back picnic with her school-district staff and I didn't want to bother her on the last day before the start of school next week. I found comfort in prayer and the kind words I received when I made several calls to some of my closest Christian brothers and sisters.

When Ruby got home I expressed my fears and discomfort. We were able to speak to doctors and nurses, both in Seattle and at Willamette Valley Cancer Center. They believed there might be fluid around my heart and urged us to go to the nearest hospital emergency room. That turned out to be Sacred Heart in Springfield

At 10 p.m., as I entered the cold, bleak and busy ER, I knew I needed to be a man with God's character. Every doctor and every nurse presented me with an opportunity to honor God, commending

"Cancer is the method God is using to put the final changes on my life. Holiness is not yet complete and He loves me enough to commit His attention to my perfection. Learning to be patient and listen to the gentle voice of the Spirit is hard work. I need to be quiet as I learn at the Savior's feet."

myself as His servant in much "...endurance, afflictions, hardships, distresses, beatings, imprisonments, tumults, labors, sleeplessness, hunger, purity, knowledge, patience, kindness, in the Holy Spirit, in genuine love, in the Word of Truth, in the power of God..."

Regardless of my fear that the next breath might be my last, I would not discredit my Lord by wavering. Yes, my future is uncertain, but I was certain was that God had called me into that ER to be His ambassador.

The last doctor at Sacred Heart to visit me administered an echo cardiogram, an ultra-sound device that showed every beat of my heart. The procedure also revealed a little bit of fluid surrounding my heart.

As the examination wand was moved around my chest, I was amazed at how fearfully and wonderfully I was made. I had nothing to fear. Just like the technician who skillfully moved the wand to show each of my heart's valves, God is skillfully moving me to new places and among new people to bring His message of hope and trust. I am still here to show much how He loves us.

Even with the fears caused by all the uncertainties this life can dish out, nothing can ever separate me from His love for me in Christ. I have an unwavering confidence in the God who will keep our heart beating until he calls us home.

It was no coincidence that the man who held the wand revealing my heart's every movement is a believer (like me); his daughter-in-law had worked at a local Christian camp (like Canyonview); and he had been married to his wife for 40 years (like Ruby and I). As we said goodnight at 1 a.m., my breathing was normal. Apart from a small amount of fluid around my heart he said there was nothing to worry about. Besides, he said, this isn't our real home anyway. So true!

After my doctor released me, Ruby and I drove home, where I slept like a baby.

As we head for Seattle, I know that we will go in the name of Christ. I get chemo and meet with my doctor tomorrow. Everywhere I go I will strive to show our Savior to this dark world. I pray that He will shine in me and through me.

September 23, 2010

You may have heard that the Creswell School Board accepted my request for unpaid leave from September 27 to December 17, 2010.

Many of you know of my husband's battle with Stage-4 cancer, which has metastasized from his right lung to his brain, to his bones (lumbar spine), and now just recently re-invaded both lungs.

We are so thankful for the thoughts and prayers people have expressed on our behalf. Recent MRIs and CAT scans have indicated that we may have less time than we had hoped. We believe that our lives are in God's hands and to worry or fret only robs us of our joy today.

In light of Dale's most recent diagnosis, we believe that we need to take some focused time for both the cancer treatments and for quality time together. Treatments will take us from Creswell to Seattle and our time together will allow us to focus on building a few more memories. Our children and grandchildren need this time with Dad and Grandpa.

With appreciation for you all, Ruby

October 4, 2010

Today we met with Dr. Martins at Seattle Cancer Care Alliance (SCCA) and got the results of the CAT scan Dale had taken early this morning. The CAT scan showed new cancerous nodules in both lungs, and indicated that the size of the previously identified nodules had increased greatly.

Dr. Martins said, "This is very disappointing and very serious. The growth of the cancer indicates that the weekly chemo treatments have not been working." Our hearts sank.

But there was more. "Things are looking grim. If we don't find a therapy that works within the next four to six months, the spread of Dale's cancer will make him pretty sick."

In some countries, there would be no further medical courses of action to take. Fortunately, we are in a country with a few additional options for us. One of those we will be able to start today. Sutent is an oral anti-cancer drug which works by reducing the blood supply of the tumors, slowing tumor growth; it is commonly used for combating kidney and liver cancer. There is no guarantee that this will work with my cancer, but Dr. Martins thinks it's the best step for now.

November 9, 2010

We just returned from Seattle after getting a brain MRI and meeting with my primary cancer doctor. The news is good, since my cancer appears to have stabilized with the new drug therapy I'm on. I do have one small tumor growing in the front part of my brain. Fortunately, it is not accompanied by any debilitating symptoms. The doctors plan to treat it with the gamma-knife radiation procedure next month, and are very hopeful of the results.

Just a month ago, Dr. Martins looked gloomy as he gave us the results showing the spread of the cancer in my lungs. After this month's examination. he smiled and said that the improvement in my condition had made his day. We walked from his office with joyous tears. The moment was far different from just a month before.

Looking back, it is easy to see how easily my emotions were swayed by the two different prognoses. I have written many times of the joy, peace, and thankfulness I experience every day when I set eyes on the One who knows my name and loves me eternally. Nonetheless, I often let my eyes drift away from the face of my one true hope. My doctors are doing all they can, but my days are still in the hands of the Great Physician.

In the past few weeks three good friends have been diagnosed with three different types of cancer. All are in serious stages but are responding well to treatment. God has used my condition and testimony to minister to them, and their strength and courage is ministering to me.

That kind of co-ministering and brotherly support reminds me of 2 Corinthians 1:3-4, where the Apostle Paul writes, "BLESSED BE THE GOD AND FATHER OF OUR LORD JESUS CHRIST, THE FATHER OF MERCIES AND GOD OF ALL COMFORT WHO COMFORTS US IN ALL OUR AFFLICTION SO THAT WE MAY BE ABLE TO COMFORT THOSE WHO ARE IN ANY AFFLICTION WITH THE COMFORT WITH WHICH WE ARE COMFORTED BY GOD."

I have always tried to be very open with people, especially about how I'm dealing with my cancer. I knew it would be easy for people to feel like, Man, what should I say to a guy with cancer? or How does Dale want me to act?, but barriers like that came down pretty quickly. I'm glad that people aren't afraid to ask me questions. I pray that my openness about my journey causes people to feel free to approach me.

Love, Dale

Jesus You're The One (Colors)
by Bill Price (Dale's younger brother)

Like a morning sun puts color in the sky
So it is with You
You bring light to our lives
You took away the darkness
That's why we want to say
Jesus, You're the one who puts the colors in each day

We're so grateful for the freedom thought You bought
Oh we could not meet the price
We could not pay the cost
Still You loosed the bonds that held our way
That's why we want to say
Jesus, You're the one who puts the colors in each day

And Jesus, we love you, we lift up our voice
And Jesus, we praise you, we lift up our voice
Jesus, you're the One
You are the One who puts the colors in each day

On and on the melody of praise goes out to You
To Thank You Lord for all you've done would be more than we could do
Oh thank You Lord

Like a morning sun puts color in the sky
So it is with You
You bring light to our lives
You took away the darkness
That's why we want to say
Jesus, You're the one who puts the colors in each day

And Jesus, we love you, we lift up our voice
And Jesus, we praise you, we lift up our voice
Jesus, you're the One
You are the One who puts the colors in each day
Jesus, You're the one who puts the colors in each day

42nd Psalm by Elaine Roemen

Chapter 7

Living in High Definition

"Every beat of my heart is in the hands of our Savior. His strength is sufficient to enable us to walk each day in His faith and hope. Please pray that nothing will distract us from the firm hope we have in Christ."

high–definition (adjective): *being or relating to an often digital television system that has twice as many scan lines per frame as a conventional system, a proportionally sharper image, and a wide-screen format*

Whether you were a longtime friend of Dale's or had just met him, "unfocused" or "indistinct" are probably not among the words you'd use to describe him. Yet Dale himself, looking back on his life before cancer, said, "In the past I was too easily distracted by the busyness of ministry and the less-important things of life. As a result, my vision was often clouded."

When Dale was diagnosed with cancer, his vision began to change as he sought God's help to enter the battle before him. Dale found he was no longer willing to see things as he had for nearly 60 years. He desired a laser-clear view of God's calling on his life and on his purpose for living.

As God began to clear and focus Dale's vision, he started seeing everything – the Lord, people, Canyonview, his cancer, the future...everything – differently. The change was radical enough to cause Dale to call his new eyesight "high definition," the perfect description for the way he wanted to live.

God's intention for every believer

More than just a slogan or attempt at trying to sound spiritual, Dale's high-definition approach helped him focus upon the truly important things in life.

AFTER JESUS anointed a blind man's eyes with mud (John 9), He told him to go to the pool of Siloam to wash. As he rinsed the mud from his eyes the man saw the physical world - for the first time ever! Later, after he had been kicked out of the temple, Jesus found him. It was then that he believed in the Son of God. When the man was able to see with brand-new spiritual eyes, he immediately worshiped Jesus.

Romans 6:3-4 describes the spiritual transformation that should be the norm for those of us who call ourselves Christians. As believers, we take our identity from Christ's death, burial, and resurrection, so we can walk with Him in newness of life. Furthermore, God gives us new sight to go along with our new life in Him.

Unfortunately, and unlike the blind man at the pool of Siloam, we often don't rinse out all the mud of our spiritual blindness, leaving us with clouded vision. Low-definition eyesight makes everything appear fuzzy. Even though we are new creations in Christ, we often operate with earthly eyes.

The Apostle Paul tells us how to see Him and our world the way God intended, praying that the "…EYES OF YOUR HEART MAY BE ENLIGHTENED, SO THAT YOU MAY KNOW THE HOPE OF HIS CALLING, WHAT ARE THE RICHES OF THE GLORY OF HIS INHERITANCE IN THE SAINTS, AND WHAT IS THE SURPASSING GREATNESS OF HIS POWER TOWARD US WHO BELIEVE" (EPHESIANS 1:18-19). In a muddied world, the clarity of high definition lets us live life like never before.

Living in high definition is what God desires for all of us. It shouldn't take a terminal illness, financial disaster or

---

"Living in high definition is what God desires for all of us. It shouldn't take a terminal illness, financial disaster or family turmoil to cause us to seek that which is both our inheritance in Christ and the best way to live."

family turmoil to cause us to seek that which is both our inheritance in Christ and the best way to live

Shortly after discovering I had cancer and wasn't expected to live long, I talked about what it meant to live in high definition. My cancer and terminal condition helped clarify my life and relationships in ways I had never experienced before. God gave me fresh eyes to see my wife, our sons and daughter-in-laws, grandsons, loving friends, and the Canyonview ministry.

IN AN article I wrote, "Six Months to Live," I talked about how being in the valley of the shadow of death helps us see that which has eternal value. That realization must lead us to live every moment God gives us as if it had eternal significance – because it does!

Living in high definition changes everything

LIFE WILL never be the same. Not just because my diagnosis might change with my next check-up, but because we are living life in high definition. Now, the value of every sunset, phone call, conversation, and walk on the beach is heightened.

I don't want life to be the same as it was before cancer. Sure, it would be wonderful to not have this disease in our lives, but God has allowed it for our good and for His eternal glory.

Last weekend I spoke to a men's-retreat group on this topic. What a blessed time, as we all dug in and learned about high-definition living from the first three chapters of Ephesians.

On Saturday, Ruby and I fly to Colorado Springs for the annual Christian Camp and Conference Association convention. At the 2008 convention I had the privilege of briefly sharing the story of our walk with Christ through my cancer diagnosis and treatment. That was a great opportunity to emphasize how our journey has put all of life into high definition.

After the convention, the leadership asked if they could use my phrase, "high definition," as the convention's theme in 2009 and if I would speak at the opening session. I quickly agreed to both requests, beginning to think even then about what God would want me to share with our camping friends in Colorado Springs the following year.

WHEN RUBY and I arrived in Colorado Springs, we found the "High-Definition" theme everywhere in the conference hall and throughout the conference program materials. As the conference progressed, person after person came up to thank us for sharing our journey of faith in such a transparent way. People we did not know revealed their own trials and losses. Some asked if they could pray for us and others asked if we would pray for them. Some just wanted to hug us and weep with us. It was overwhelming.

On the third day of the conference we ate lunch with a dear couple from a camp in Michigan. While we were sharing, God answered my prayer for a consciousness of His presence.

I realized that we were in the presence of God. He had sent this couple to minister to us, with their hands, hearts, and hugs. Christ, the Word of God, certainly "became flesh and dwelt among us" during that lunch. These friends and hundreds of others are the Body of Christ ministering to us. God's Spirit dwells within them and within us.

It is as the Apostle John writes, "... IF WE WALK IN THE LIGHT, AS HE IS IN THE LIGHT, WE HAVE FELLOWSHIP WITH ONE ANOTHER AND THE BLOOD OF JESUS HIS SON CLEANSES US FROM ALL SIN" (1 JOHN 1:7). Fellowship means communion, to share in common, or to be in community together with one another and with God.

JESUS DESCRIBED this wonderful mystery of fellowship and communion to His disciples when He said, "WHENEVER TWO OR THREE OF ARE GATHERED TOGETHER IN MY NAME I AM IN THEIR MIDST" (MATTHEW 18:20). Over and over, I witnessed God's presence in the midst of our fellowship at the CCCA conference. It was then that I realized God had been revealing Himself everywhere I turned. His is not a hypothetical or conceptual presence, but an abiding, transcendent, comforting, convicting, and helping presence.

Many of you have acted as God's agents toward us and one another as you have phoned, sent cards, and written in the CaringBridge guestbook. Our family, our home church in Silverton, the Canyonview Camp family, pastors in Silverton and Creswell, and the broader family of Christian camping throughout the world have reached out with God's hands to comfort and support us.

WITH A deep appreciation and sense of blessing, I see God's presence in the fellowship of believers. The Apostle Paul ends his second epistle to the Corinthians with this prayer, "THE GRACE OF THE LORD JESUS CHRIST, AND THE LOVE OF GOD, AND THE FELLOWSHIP OF THE HOLY SPIRIT, BE WITH YOU ALL." I can ask for nothing more. Thank you for loving me and my family.

One of my common (and favorite) answers to the question, "What's been happening with you, Dale?" is this: Jesus grabbed my hand and lifted me out of the green pastures and beyond the still waters where I'd been before cancer crashed into my world. Together, my Lord and I walked hand in hand into the valley of the shadow of death. Yes, that valley.

God uses tribulation to develop our character, so we need the valleys to teach us patience, endurance, and long-suffering. Gaining those vital spiritual characteristics, however, rarely happens in the green pastures or still waters or a comfortable life.

I have been given a course to finish, but cannot do it in my own strength. Christ is in the lead and He must guide me to the finish line. During the times when I feel better, it is easy to forget how desperately I must depend on the power of the One who holds me up (and also on the prayers of each of you as you make your requests to God on my behalf).

A few years ago I was completing my first marathon and had just 385 yards to go. When I saw the finish-line banner all my weariness slipped away. With my eyes on the goal, I could not only make it to the end, I could sprint the rest of the way!. Cancer has brought my personal finish line into view. Arriving there may take months or years, but journeying in high definition helps make the cares of this world fade away.

Paul states that he kept the faith. If anyone had a reason to question the "good" part of the Good News it was the Apostle Paul. He was beaten, imprisoned, shipwrecked, mocked and eventually killed because he was true to the faith. His confidence in God's truth grew stronger with every trial.

I pray that I will follow that pattern. I want to join Peter in claiming that the testing and proof of my faith is truly "MORE PRECIOUS THAN GOLD" (1 PETER 1:7).

GOD HAS been teaching me so much about living a high-definition life, helping me see this world with the eyes of truth, faith, and hope. These are spiritual eyes and they are not of this world.

If you want to know more about what God has been teaching me regarding high-definition vision, read about the newly created man of 2 Corinthians 5:17; the man walking in newness of life (Romans 6:4); and the man who sees with the eyes of the heart (Ephesians 1:18-23).

I pray we never lose the passion to live life in high definition. God sends divine encounters every day that bless us – if we choose to see them. The most amazing experience in this life is to find yourself in God's hand, doing His work in the lives of others.

Divine appointments

EVERY DAY is a gift from God and life in high definition gives me God-ordained opportunities to serve Him. Ruby and I are blessed as we share with others about God's faithfulness in the midst of suffering. We are thankful children of God, who have been blessed with every spiritual blessing.

YESTERDAY I shared our testimony with the brothers and sisters in a small church here in Creswell. They were just starting a new church-wide program called, "Thirty Days to Live," and our testimony helped kick off their first full week of commitment.

I shared briefly with them some of the Apostle Paul's words toward the end of 2 Timothy. "FOR I AM ALREADY BEING POURED OUT AS A DRINK OFFERING AND THE TIME OF MY DEPARTURE HAS COME. I HAVE FOUGHT THE GOOD FIGHT, I HAVE FINISHED THE COURSE, I HAVE KEPT THE FAITH; IN THE FUTURE THERE IS LAID UP FOR ME THE CROWN OF RIGHTEOUS-NESS, WHICH THE LORD, THE RIGHTEOUS JUDGE WILL AWARD TO ME ON THAT DAY; AND NOT ONLY TO ME, BUT ALSO TO ALL

WHO HAVE LOVED HIS APPEARING." 2 TIMOTHY 4:6-8

We don't know how many days or weeks or even months Paul lived after he penned these words. It is obvious, however, that he was living with a clear sense of purpose. There was a fight to fight, a course to finish and a faith to keep.

AS I enter this stage of our battle I realize that the fight for physical life is not what Paul is speaking of here. The fight is for the truth of the Gospel. My cancer has given me a fresh battlefield, but it is the same fight I've been in since I gave my life to Christ more than 50 years ago.

There is a difference, though, between my fight before and after the cancer diagnosis. Because of that earth-shattering event and God's precious gift to me of a high-definition life, I believe I have greater clarity than I have ever had. My time on earth may be shorter than I imagined, but I have a renewed sense of urgency.

Psalm 63:5-8 becomes more precious to me as I move forward in the journey, keeping my (high-definition) eyes on God. I'm safe under His wings, singing for joy, confident in His care.

"MY SOUL IS SATISFIED AS WITH MARROW AND FATNESS, AND MY MOUTH OFFERS PRAISES WITH JOYFUL LIPS.

WHEN I REMEMBER YOU ON MY BED, I MEDITATE ON YOU IN THE NIGHT WATCHES,

FOR YOU HAVE BEEN MY HELP, AND IN THE SHADOW OF YOUR WINGS I SING FOR JOY.

MY SOUL CLINGS TO YOU; YOUR RIGHT HAND UPHOLDS ME."

Living in God's timeframe, not mine

WHAT WILL tomorrow hold? Someone knows the answer to that question, but that someone isn't me!

We've been praying we would hear words from the doctors like, "This is the best possible outcome we could have hoped for!" or "The gamma-knife treatment worked so well, the tumors in your brain have been destroyed and there is no new cancer activity in your lungs!" We also know we may hear words like, "Your results are not positive."

Thousands of people are praying for us throughout the world; we have an outstanding team of doctors, nurses, and medical technicians; and, best of all, Great Physician is in charge of everything.

We wait on the Lord and strive to have His patience, placing our trust in His will and in His timing. Having patience is difficult and inseparably linked to trust. All of us want to know God's will and we want to know it now! However, God tells us to be patient and then gifts us with His Holy Spirit so we can patiently wait for Him to reveal His perfect plan.

I can't achieve this kind of patience in my own strength, but I need not despair. All I need to do is pray and make my requests known to Him. "BE ANXIOUS FOR NOTHING, BUT IN EVERYTHING BY PRAYER SUPPLICATION WITH THANKSGIVING..." We have made our requests known to Him again and again, and the peace He promised us floods in, just like He said it would.

Learning patience (as well as actually practicing it!) is hard work. I need Him every hour and must abide in Jesus, the true vine. Only then does patience come; only there does my heart find peace and rest.

One of the sweetest things I've learned since my diagnosis is dependency upon God. When I place all my needs before Him I learn what it means to rely on and trust Him alone. What does my dependency on Him look like? It begins with abiding in Christ, savoring the constant communion I can have in His presence.

My job as a cancer patient isn't just to stay alive. As a Christian (who happens to have cancer), I have a greater calling and job, with an even greater payoff than just surviving. My job right now is to stay in Christ, walk with Him, stay with Him and find my all in Him.

Focusing on our unknown future in this unstable world only leads to fear and uncertainty. However, focusing on what God is accomplishing right here, right now, gives us joy because we have confidence in God's abiding love.

THE MOST important message we must understand is that God is faithful. He gives us His comfort every day and provides all we need to live a high-definition life with a clear sense of purpose.

Of course, we don't know what is around the corner; none of us do. But that is why it is called "walking by faith!" When our trust in Christ goes beyond our salvation, we can have the faith and desire to place our trust in Him. When we put every moment, every person, every day, every fear and every cell in His perfect care, that's when we can rest.

I have prayed since we left Seattle that God would, once

"One of the sweetest things I've learned since my diagnosis is dependency upon God. When I place all my needs before Him I learn what it means to rely on and trust Him alone. What does my dependency on Him look like? It begins with abiding in Christ, savoring the constant communion I can have in His presence."

more, give me peace. Not just any kind of peace, but the kind that only comes when I trust in His lovingkindness toward me and my family. He has answered my prayers (no surprise there!) and I want to share what I have learned from my Savior. Some are lessons He's patiently taught me before, but ones I needed God's Spirit to remind me of once again.

He knows my days. The prognosis doctors deliver or the odds of my survival do not control my future – God does. I will have the exact number of days He has ordained for me, no less and no more. Worry or anxiousness only robs me of the joy He wants to give me today.

He loves me and He loves my family. Honestly, I can't help but be concerned about how my family will endure when the Lord calls me home. However, I have no control over the days that have not yet come; as Husband, Dad, and Grandpa, I can only impact today. I pray that my family will find a legacy of faith, hope and love that lasts long after I am gone.

He is the One in whom I'll rejoice: "REJOICE IN THE LORD ALWAYS; AGAIN I WILL SAY REJOICE" (PHILIPPIANS 4:4). To rejoice is a decision. More to the point, it's my choice whether or not to rejoice in Him.

In Psalm 102, David is in despair, crying out to God and asking Him not to hide His face. The pain continues as David laments, "MY DAYS ARE CONSUMED IN SMOKE, AND MY BONES HAVE BEEN SCORCHED LIKE A HEARTH."

I identify with David's plea to God. I have discovered, as David expresses later in that Psalm, that the only antidote to despair is the righteous, faithful, and loving character of God. In the very next Psalm, David's confidence, rooted in God's sufficiency, compels him to write, "BLESS THE LORD, O MY SOUL, AND FORGET NONE OF HIS BENEFITS; WHO PARDONS ALL YOUR INIQUITIES, WHO HEALS ALL YOUR

DISEASES, WHO REDEEMS YOUR LIFE FROM THE PIT, WHO CROWNS YOU WITH LIVING KINDNESS AND COMPASSION."

As I learn more about my relationship with the Lord I find He has given me a fresh, high-definition view of the 23rd Psalm. Verse 5 says, "YOU PREPARE A TABLE BEFORE ME IN THE PRESENCE OF MY ENEMIES; YOU HAVE ANOINTED MY HEAD WITH OIL; MY CUP OVERFLOWS."

HERE'S THE picture I see: I'm walking hand in hand with my Savior as He leads me into the valley of the shadow of death. He selects a spot along the rugged path, stops and begins preparing a meal for us to share. He sets the table and we dine together, just my Savior and me.

All around us I see signs of the Enemy. He has been watching our pathway through this threatening valley, but the Savior's presence has thwarted any potential attacks.

As we dine I am at peace and safe. His rod and staff are comforting, but my deepest comfort comes from His presence. I am not afraid, which must drive the Enemy nuts!

HE DECLARES that I am his child forever and that nothing will ever separate me from His love. Then, He blesses me with the anointing. The touch of His fingers on my head is amazing! It's the touch of my Lord's commitment to my eternal and present well-being.

As He fills my cup I see that it's the cup of communion, filled with His sufferings. This cup of the new covenant is overflowing with spiritual blessings. Thankfully, He doesn't hold back, so my life, in its turn, overflows with gratitude and wonder as He keeps pouring into my cup of blessing.

NOW, I see how the valley-of-the-shadow fits in this picture. I am like the horses, sheep and other animals that scatter when threatened; my emotions can urge me to run when I fear the unknown. For example, when Ruby and I meet with my doctor I don't know what we'll hear. Whether it is today or a day in the future, there will probably be another unwelcome diagnosis like we received 19 months ago.

I will not live in fear. He has set a table before me and I am dining with Him. The Enemy can rage all around me, but Christ has already won the battle. He calms my fears and we dine in peace and sweet fellowship.

Times of testing, teaching, thanks giving

AS I prepare to share at the city of Creswell's community Thanksgiving service, I wonder how different this season would have been if the doctor's reports had been different. Would we still be filled with His praise? I pray we would.

I pray that our physical circumstances will never overshadow the joy God gives through His Spirit. He has given us life - His life - so we might exist to the praise of His glorious grace forever.

"BLESSED BE THE GOD AND FATHER OF OUR LORD JESUS CHRIST WHO HAS BLESSED US WITH EVERY SPIRITUAL BLESSING IN THE HEAVENLY PLACES IN CHRIST." EPHESIANS 1:3

AS YOU can imagine, these days are filled with testing for us. I confess that fear and worry try to creep in and capture my mind, yet God's Spirit within me is greater than my emotions and He sets my mind free to trust Him. He is greater than any terror this world (or my diagnosis) throws at me.

When I'm afraid and don't know whether the news about my fight with cancer will be terrible, bad or good, I run to Jesus, seek His face, and concentrate on how much he loves me and Ruby and our family. Thank you for fighting alongside us with your prayers. The battle for my frail life continues, but the battle for our eternity has already been won through the cross of Christ. We rest in Him.

DAVID'S EXHORTATION to "forget none of His benefits" is the key to my present joy. He has loved me, redeemed me and has an eternal future for me. The past 14 months have included countless benefits that I'll never forget. From my teaching and counseling opportunities in Russia, to the birth of my fourth grandson, and ministry in Creswell, we have received so many blessings/benefits. Nearly every day God allows me to tell someone the story of His faithfulness and what it means to abide in Him.

"I THANK MY GOD IN ALL MY REMEMBRANCE OF YOU, ALWAYS OFFERING PRAYER WITH JOY IN MY EVERY PRAYER FOR YOU ALL, IN VIEW OF YOUR PARTICIPATION IN THE GOSPEL FROM THE FIRST DAY UNTIL NOW. FOR I AM CONFIDENT OF THIS VERY THING, THAT HE WHO BEGAN A GOOD WORK IN YOU WILL PERFECT IT UNTIL THE DAY OF CHRIST JESUS." PHILIPPIANS 1:3-6

ON EASTER morning, a few hours before we left for Seattle I spoke at the sunrise service about what it means to live each day in the power of the resurrection. Some of the things I've been learning are especially powerful in my life right now, serving to stabilize me in the midst of my stormy seas.

At Easter we celebrate the most profound event that ever touched this world. Sin and its eternal effects were conquered when Jesus was raised from the dead.

Romans 6:5-11 says we have become inseparably linked to the death, burial and resurrection or Christ. Our old,

> *"I identify with David's plea to God. I have discovered, as David expresses later in that Psalm, that the only antidote to despair is the righteous, faithful, and loving character of God."*

sin-dominated self was crucified with Him. Those who have died with Him, by placing their faith in the salvation Christ provides, shall also live with Him. Forever.

Verse 11 challenges those of us who have been raised with Christ to consider ourselves as alive to God. Just as Christ was raised from the dead through the glory of the Father, we too should walk in newness of life.

BUT, WHAT does the resurrection of Christ have to do with our lives today? Is it more than looking back to events that took place so many years ago? Is it more than something we look forward to in the future? Does it change, inspire and empower me today, while I'm still in this body and on this planet?

At Easter we celebrate the most profound and transformational event that ever touched this world. Sin and its eternal effects were conquered as Jesus was raised from the dead.

The response of the disciples and others on that first Easter teaches us a lot about our own responses to Christ's conquering of the grace. Which of the resurrection appearances is my favorite?

- The women arriving in grief at dawn, encountering angels and finding their mourning turned to joy.
- John and Peter racing to the tomb to verify what the women had seen.

- The angels displaying an empty tomb and declaring the bodily resurrection of Jesus.
- Jesus appearing to Mary (after she mistakes Him for the gardener).
- Christ materializing among the disciples, both with and without Thomas.
- Jesus travelling the road to Emmaus, enflaming the hearts of two disciples.
- The seaside breakfast, with Jesus cooking fish for His disciples.

Be sure to remember all these amazing testimonies as we celebrate the fact that death could not keep Jesus in the grave. He is alive! He is risen!

THERE IS transforming, resurrection power going on every moment, even though we are still encased in these humble bodies. Our resurrection with Christ gives us new minds, as we continue to be renewed into the likeness of Christ's mind. Because we're new creations in Christ we've been given new, high-definition eyes so we can clearly see the spiritual things of this life.

According to Ephesians. 2, we are not only made alive together with Christ but have already been raised with Him and seated with Him in the heavenlies. Our heavenly resurrection and position in Jesus is secure, even while we're still living here.

Like anything worth giving our lives to, living a resurrected life comes with a cost. We no longer live for ourselves but for the One who died on our behalf and rose from the grave. Our lives belong to Him. But, praise God, it is only in Him that we find genuine purpose, direction, joy, peace, and security.

We don't walk this resurrection life alone. I can live each

day knowing that it belongs to God. Striving and fear are gone. I can say with the Apostle Paul in Philippians 3 that my goal is "...TO KNOW HIM AND THE POWER OF HIS RESUR-RECTION AND THE FELLOWSHIP OF HIS SUFFERINGS, BEING CONFORMED TO HIS DEATH, WITH THE ULTIMATE ATTAINMENT BEING THE RESURRECTION FROM THE DEAD."

We hope in a future resurrection, too, when we will behold Him in His glory and become transformed into the same image, from glory to glory. The power of the resurrection shines in us and we are like stars in this dark world.

RUBY AND I are facing the very real possibility that the duration of my life on earth may be far shorter than we anticipated. It's easy for any of us to buy into the illusion that we're somehow guaranteed a long life. When we expect to have years and years and years ahead of us, we tend to think, "Hey, I've got lots of time to reorder my priorities, correct my decisions, communicate love or truth to those who need them, or even just to enjoy sunsets and grandkids."

I have been studying in Mark 12 and want to share what the Holy Spirit has been teaching my mind and heart through this Scripture.

When we live as if we have lots of time left, we usually give God the leftovers - that which we consider surplus, extra, non-essential. The story of the widow in Mark 12 is the story of an impoverished (and probably uneducated) woman who knew more than all the Scribes and Pharisees who had been questioning Jesus. She understood that all she had in her present life belonged to God and that all the questions about her future life were secure in His hands.

What is the difference in our hearts and minds – not to mention in our actions - when we give to God out of our surplus instead of our essence? We retain control when we look at what we have (or think we have) as our excess. The results? We don't have to trust anyone but ourselves.

What happens to our minds and hearts and actions when we give God all we have? Does this supposed loss of control scare us? Or give us peace? The peace we long for becomes ours when we know and absolutely trust the One to whom we have given everything.

When I consider my own weak life as but two copper coins, I wonder if God will grant me more coins. Do I allow Him to only possess just the two, while I retain ownership over the rest, to do with it as I choose? Or, as the widow understood, do I give my entire life/all my coins to Him, trusting Him with my future?

PROBABLY THE most important lesson I am learning these days is how to have patience.

From Romans 5:3-5, we know that tribulation produces patience. I always rush through these three verses so I can get to the part about proven character and hope.

Becoming patient is really tough for me. Living through day after nauseous day is a battle I never thought I would fight. Feeling sick (because of the side effects of my cancer treatments) is like facing an invisible enemy who knows exactly how to torment, weaken and discourage me. Mealtimes aren't good and there is no joy in sitting down to eat with friends or family. Do I sound like I'm whining? I hope not.

Patience begins with trusting God. Can I trust that He will give me the strength I need, especially during those times when I have none?

HE KNOWS exactly what I can handle, but it's the waiting part of patience that is so hard. In my flesh I want God to answer my prayers immediately! But that's not patience. So I wait and trust, resting on His unchanging and all-sufficient grace, learning to practice patience.

I must recount a few things God has taught me over the last couple of days. They have given me both comfort and hope, sufficient for the journey.

1. While preaching at church last Sunday God re-impressed on me the amazing truth and command to be patient. This life doesn't lack opportunities to practice being patient. Father, help us have patience with the circumstances of and people affected by worldwide strife, unrelenting attacks on God's truth, an unwelcome cancer diagnosis, enduring unrelenting pain, God's timing, and more.

We're told in James 5 to be patient until the coming of the Lord. Verse 8 says, "YOU TOO BE PATIENT, STRENGTHEN YOUR HEARTS, FOR THE COMING OF THE LORD IS AT HAND."

God's timing is perfect and He will strengthen me to carry any load at any time. Satan is trying to use my current pain to make me impatient with God and His timing. Unfortunately, my fleshly nature always wants answers today. God is in control and He will reveal His perfect plan at the perfect time. The nausea and pain I have now is part of

---

"When I consider my own weak life as but two copper coins, I wonder if God will grant me more coins. Do I allow Him to only possess just the two, while I retain ownership over the rest, to do with it as I choose? Or, as the widow understood, do I give my entire life/all my coins to Him, trusting Him with my future?"

---

the method God is using to make me more and more like Him.

2. While having lunch with a friend at a small restaurant in Silverton, a man and his wife approached me (they must have heard my too-loud voice of praise for what God is doing and teaching!) and asked about my cancer. We chatted and shared email addresses and phone numbers. He is part of a cancer-survivor support group, and he asked if I would speak at one of their upcoming meetings.

God is not done with me! He keeps adding to my to-do list. My pain is not in vain and I will try to never waste these opportunities.

I am enjoying a week without chemo. I feel pretty normal – not much pain and no new symptoms. Last Sunday I was blessed to preach at a local Silverton church and was able to build on the pastor's prior message about the first and greatest commandment, "YOU SHALL LOVE THE LORD YOUR GOD WITH ALL YOUR HEART, WITH ALL YOUR SOUL, AND WITH ALL YOUR STRENGTH...."

THE PASTOR asked me to focus my remarks on the phrase "all your strength," something I was glad to do, since I have written in my journal many times about the loss of my physical strength over the course of my battle with cancer.

The commandment is not referring to physical strength, (except to point out that if you've got it, then use it with all your might to serve God and bring Him glory). I continue to find strength to serve my Savior in every way He asks. What I now lack in physical strength has been replaced by a spiritual strength in my inner man. Paul prays in Ephesians 3:16, "THAT HE WOULD GRANT YOU, ACCORDING TO THE RICHES OF HIS GLORY, TO BE STRENGTHENED WITH POWER THROUGH HIS SPIRIT IN THE INNER MAN."

If this inner strengthening by the Spirit is not the ongoing work of God, then aging, sickness, and physical disability will produce great despair. The blessed truth, however, is that in our weakness we can experience the power of God within us! We also have the privilege of being the living demonstration and testimony of that power. He has chosen us for this mission. I closed with the words of the Lord to the Apostle Paul: "MY GRACE IS SUFFICIENT FOR YOU FOR POWER IS PERFECTED IN WEAKNESS" (2 CORINTHIANS 12:9).

I don't know what is around the corner but I do know that His strength will be sufficient. I pray that my story will always be about Him, not me.

The transforming power of high definition

I PRAY that this will be a year of transformation for you. I pray also that it will be a year of living in high definition, so you can see and experience - in new and powerful ways - the joy and peace and power of abiding in Christ!

The word "new" is a powerful word and theme as used in the Bible.

- "THROUGH CHRIST I HAVE BECOME A NEW CREATURE." 2 CORINTHIANS 5:17

- In Colossians 3 we "...HAVE LAID ASIDE THE OLD SELF WITH ITS EVIL PRACTICES AND HAVE PUT ON THE NEW SELF WHO IS BEING RENEWED TO A TRUE KNOWLEDGE ACCORDING TO THE IMAGE OF THE ONE WHO CREATED HIM."

- Ephesians 4:23-24 tells us we are, by God's power, "...RENEWED IN THE SPIRIT OF YOUR MIND, AND PUT ON THE NEW SELF, WHICH IN THE LIKENESS OF GOD HAS BEEN CREATED IN RIGHTEOUSNESS AND HOLINESS OF THE TRUTH."

- Finally, something I'm reminded of every day when I look in the mirror: "THEREFORE WE DO NOT LOSE HEART, BUT THOUGH OUR OUTER MAN IS DECAYING,

YET OUR INNER MAN IS BEING RENEWED DAY BY DAY."
2 CORINTHIANS 4:16

PRAYER HAS been an intimate part of our lives this past year. I certainly prayed with Jesus that God would take this cup (cancer) out of my life. But I have always finished that prayer, as Jesus did, with, "Nevertheless, not my will but Your will be done."

I know it is the will of God for me to be alive today, and He has placed His Word in my heart and in my mind. It is His will that I declare His salvation as long as He gives me breath.

I have written before that I will not live one day less nor one day longer than my Creator desires. But some days, when I think of my wife, our sons and their wives, our grandsons, and all the rest of our family and church family, it is hard not to wonder about the length of my days here.

I struggle to agree with the Apostle Paul that it is better to depart and be with the Lord. Heaven is filled with so many unknowns while life on this little speck of dirt in the middle of this vast universe has been my only home, and it is filled with people I love and people who love me.

I have chosen to trust God with everything about my life, including leaving here for heaven. There we will have perfect fellowship with Him - for eternity. We will have sinless and perfect fellowship with one another, also for eternity. As I pray, I am thanking God for all of you who are praying for me and my family. I am thanking God that it is September and He has chosen to let me be with you all for a while more, and I am thanking God that when He takes my home His timing will be perfect.

THIS JOURNEY with Christ has never been dull, but it is now more wonderfully intense than I have ever previously experienced. I believe this is because my old (unredeemed) man is being increasingly replaced by the new man I am in Christ. This is the work God intends to do in me through tribulation (Romans 5), discipline (Hebrews 12), and His refining fire (1 Peter 1).

I am humbled by the fact that He had to use this much testing and heat to produce the ongoing transformation I need. At the same time, I am blessed that He loves me enough to grant me His master-craftsman attention.

The CaringBridge connection

Col. Price, I wish you a most happy Veteran's Day! It was such a delight to see you and Ruby at the 104D retiree reunion! You both looked great! I read each of your diary entries and always look forward to your words of wisdom and inspiration. You are in our thoughts and prayers.

Seeing you and Ruby at the Canyonview auction/dinner made it that much more special. It was great watching the two of you dance; it brought a tear to my eye. Both of you are an inspiration to me and so many others. Thanks for all you do for Canyonview. The camp and its ministry has made me a better man; been great for my kids; and is a special place for my family.

What a joy it was to see you and Ruby in Coeur d'Alene and have a chance to share a couple of meals with you. Your influence on the Christian Camp and Conference Association in Oregon, and worldwide, is amazing.

Ruby, thank you for being my dear sister and friend! You bless me every time we talk over the phone. I love that we can call any time and just resume our conversation, sharing deeply from our hearts.

Thanks for being my devoted sister and my caring confidante. I just read Romans 8:38-39 and am encouraged by Paul's words: "FOR I AM CONVINCED THAT NEITHER DEATH, NOR LIFE, NOR ANGELS, NOR PRINCIPALITIES, NOR THINGS PRESENT, NOR THINGS TO COME, NOR POWERS, NOR HEIGHT, NOR DEPTH, NOR ANY OTHER CREATED THING, SHALL BE ABLE TO SEPARATE US FROM THE LOVE OF GOD WHICH IS IN CHRIST JESUS." May you both feel His presence and His great love for you at this moment.

"I am humbled by the fact that He had to use this much testing and heat to produce the ongoing transformation I need. At the same time, I am blessed that He loves me enough to grant me His master-craftsman attention."

STEP BY STEP

January 9, 2011

Dale has an MRI and CAT scan, and then they meet with their team of doctors. They will stay in Seattle for a few days so Dale can get some recovery time. Each course of chemotherapy course has a number of side effects, but the current treatments have affected Dale's tongue so that it hurts when he tries to eat. Consequently, Dale has lost some weight, which he needs to gain back.

January 9, 2011

As we enter this New Year, I am rejoicing that God continues to give me life and hope and purpose.

About two months ago, my MRIs showed had two small tumors in my brain. In addition to that, the CAT scan of my lungs showed active growth of the cancer in both lungs. My oncologist in Seattle had planned for a gamma-knife procedure on my brain in early December, but delayed the procedure because of the slowed growth of the cancer in both the brain and lung.

My symptoms have improved since mid-December, so I am excited to see if the tests will show the same kind of improvements in the fight to eliminate the cancer.

Thank you for your prayers as I continue in this earthly tent knowing that God is preparing a new heavenly tent for me which will be eternal in heaven.

January 12, 2011

I've resigned my position as superintendent of the Creswell Schools.

The grief I feel in saying goodbye to this wonderful community has been very real. The pain and regret of unfinished dreams is intense. Yet I know God has set aside this time for Dale and me. It is a time of much more than fighting cancer. It's a time of closeness for us as a couple that's unlike any we've ever had. And, it's a time I won't get to do over again.

Either I will be here to care for, support and love my husband through the next unknown steps or I won't. I am learning to surrender to each moment, to live in the reality of that moment.

January 13, 2011

I am sitting in the waiting room at Harborview Hospital in Seattle where Dale in undergoing the gamma-knife procedure on the tumors in his brain. I know we are living a miracle and the prayers of our family and friends are being answered daily. Dale continues to live victoriously and fully, despite the lung cancer that has metastasized to his brain and bones.

People tell me I am brave, but there is much they don't see or know. Only God and I know that I hang onto my sanity by just a thread. It feels like every step I take is along the edge of a precipice; one step to either side or one slip, and I will fall and never recover.

The neurosurgeon has just come back into the waiting room. The gamma-knife surgery was successful! They were able to target all 10 new cancerous lesions from more than 200 different angles, pinpointing each tumor for destruction.

March 3, 2011

As Ruby and I traveled to Seattle Cancer Care Alliance we didn't know what the appointments would reveal. We hoped the news would be good, allowing me to qualify for the experimental treatment plan that had been discussed in January.

But what we hoped for was not in God's plan.

At least three additional tumors had grown in my head since our last appointment, immediately disqualifying me from the new, experimental therapy.

With tears in our eyes, Ruby and I let this unwanted news sink in, thanking God for the ministry opportunities He continues to give us. I keep praying, asking God to reveal His purpose in all these miraculous events.

April 2, 2011

You are all very much in Dale and Ruby's heart. They want you to know what is going on.

Your prayers are needed more than ever. The cancer is threatening Dale's brain, but he is determined to keep fighting. Pray that he will be able to eat and gain physical strength. Pray that the good brain cells will be spared and only the cancerous cells will be obliterated. Dale and Ruby continue walking with the Lord every step of the way, seeking to bring Him glory.

Ruby and I returned from Seattle last Thursday with challenging but hopeful news. The cancer in my lungs has remained steady, but the cancer in my brain is growing exponentially. We will return to Seattle Cancer Care Alliance on April 3 to continue this fight against cancer. I will begin two weeks of whole-brain radiation on Tuesday. There is some risk involved, but my life has always been in my Lord's hands. Whether this part of the journey will be long or a short, it is what we believe the Lord has for us.

April 10, 2011

Ruby and Dale send their greetings and are grateful for your prayers. Ruby said she can feel the supernatural power surrounding them that comes from your prayers. "Be anxious for nothing, and in everything give thanks" is still on Dale and Ruby's lips, even as they're sitting in the hospital this afternoon getting an IV for Dale.

They were able to spend a blessed weekend with their son and daughter-in-law, Josh and Jennifer, and grandsons, Cody and Tyler. They all went up in the Space Needle and, after viewing Seattle from the observation deck, they celebrated Ruby's birthday at their favorite Italian restaurant.

Dale is having a lot of unexplained, unanticipated pain. It's not from the whole-brain radiation. (Those side effects had been planned for and dealt with.) The pain, which has been debilitating at times, is in Dale's stomach and saps his strength. Please pray for an end to the stomach pain, that radiation stops the brain cancer and for Dale's physical strength.

Please pray with us. Dale's brain cancer and treatments have hindered his ability to put a sentence together. This is a very frustrating complication, since Dale loves to communicate with people, especially about Christ. Dale's passion for his entire life has been teaching the Gospel. He is a talented Bible teacher who has impacted the lives of thousands of children and adults, and it's very hard to see Dale unable to use his gifts fully. Keep praying, friends.

April 15, 2011

During the night, Dale was rushed by ambulance to a hospital in Seattle. He has a serious lung infection and it is difficult for him to breathe. Matt and Amy were already in Seattle, visiting for the weekend, and Josh and Jennifer are on their way. The situation is very serious, but Dale and Ruby are at peace and unafraid.

EVERY BEAT of my heart is in the hands of our Savior. His strength is sufficient to enable us to walk each day in His faith and hope. Please pray that nothing will distract us from the firm hope we have in Christ. "THIS HOPE WE HAVE AS AN ANCHOR OF THE SOUL, A HOPE BOTH SURE AND STEADFAST." HEBREWS 6:19

When my strength fails, His strength is more than sufficient to carry me. It's in Him alone that we stand through the fiercest of trials. "MY FLESH AND MY HEART MAY FAIL, BUT GOD IS THE STRENGTH OF MY HEART AND MY PORTION FOREVER." PSALM 73:26

What have I learned in the last two and a half years?

God loves me, He knows my name and there is nothing hidden from His sight. He alone is writing His to-do list on my heart and giving me the strength to do all He asks.

What is my expectation for this life?

That I will live no longer and no shorter than God ordains for me. That for every day He gives me He will prepare a can-do list for me.

From the moment I wake up until the moment I fall asleep, my life is in His hands. It does me no good to worry or fret. Ruby and I have entrusted our lives to our Redeemer and Savior, and seek our peace from only Him.

Please pray with us that we will keep our minds fixed on Him, fulfilling His call on our lives and following Paul's instructions, "SET YOUR MIND ON THE THINGS ABOVE, NOT ON THE THINGS THAT ARE ON EARTH" (COLOSSIANS 3:2), and reaching towards the "PRIZE OF THE UPWARD CALL OF GOD IN CHRIST JESUS" (PHILIPPIANS 3:14).

Chapter 8

The Dad We Always Wanted

"If you want to really worship God, there's no better place to be than on a mountaintop or in a deep forest, surrounded by His creation."

For Dale and Ruby's sons, Matt and Josh, some of the greatest words they'll ever hear are the words that simultaneously
honor their dad's life and remind them of their own desire
to follow in his footsteps. When someone asks one of them,
"You're Dale Price's son, aren't you?" or says, "You're just like
your dad." they couldn't be more pleased.

Josh and Matt not only know their father is the greatest
influence in their earthly lives, they are willing to share the
reasons why. [Note: Although the first-person, singular "I" is
used below, both men contributed content for this chapter.]

*Even though it is so hard for us to lose an amazing man like
my dad, he left a wonderful example of how we should live our
lives to glorify Christ. He did so much and truly used all of his
gifts and energy for God's glory.*

*To us, he always was larger than life. When we were kids,
our family went to Disneyland. We had to see Mickey Mouse, of
course, so we went running up to him yelling, "Mickey! Mickey!"
and got a big hug.*

*Just a few minutes later, some other kids ran up, but they
went straight to Dad! They started yelling, "Buzzard, Buzzard!"
Yes, in his own way and to the people who loved him, he was
a celebrity. Introductions have always been easy; all I need to
say is, "Hi, I'm Dale's son. You know, Buzzard?"*

*If you knew Dad, you know he loved the outdoors. "If you
want to really worship God," he said, "there's no better place
to be than on a mountaintop or in a deep forest, surrounded
by His creation."*

*Whenever we walked in the woods, whether on a wilderness
backpack trip or just at Canyonview, he'd point out a tree or
hill as if they were longtime friends of his. Which they were, I
guess, because he knew them so well and spent so much time
with them. He taught us to stop and listen to the birds, as well
as the silence.*

*He shared his awe of creation with others whenever he could.
Many camp days would begin with everyone gathered around*

the flag pole and Dad reading from the Bible. A favorite passage for those times was Psalm 104:10-13:

HE SENDS FORTH SPRINGS IN THE VALLEYS;
THEY FLOW BETWEEN THE MOUNTAINS;
THEY GIVE DRINK TO EVERY BEAST OF THE FIELD;
THE WILD DONKEYS QUENCH THEIR THIRST.

Dad loved nature, but it was more than just the beauty and recreation. He loved the way nature displayed God's glory and creativity. He often referred to Romans 1:20 when describing how the Lord's handiwork reveals who He is:

FOR SINCE THE CREATION OF THE WORLD HIS INVISIBLE ATTRIBUTES, HIS ETERNAL POWER AND DIVINE NATURE, HAVE BEEN CLEARLY SEEN, BEING UNDERSTOOD THROUGH WHAT HAS BEEN MADE, SO THAT THEY ARE WITHOUT EXCUSE.

Dad instilled in us a strong sense of exploration and adventure. That made sense, considering that after high school, he traveled through Europe on bicycle. During his college years, he and his brother, Jim, made trips on motorcycles. He and Mom had all sorts of adventures during the years they lived in Germany.

After that, at Canyonview, he led countless bike trips in Canada, backpacking trips, sailing trips, and high-adventure trips. No matter where he was or who he was with, the hardships and challenges they encountered were both an adventure and an opportunity to share about Jesus Christ.

I can only imagine the adventures he's having now! My son has been asking a lot of questions about heaven and what it's like there. I'm wondering the same thing. I have a feeling it's going to be a whole other world, filled with mountains, forests, rivers, and oceans, just waiting to be explored. One of the first things Dad probably asked when he got there was, "Could I get a topographical map? I'd really like to plan a trip."

Dad's pursuit and enjoyment of outdoor activities was something he did all his life, almost until his last days. Even after he was diagnosed with cancer, he still enjoyed snowboarding and many other activities. He didn't always feel his best, but he rarely complained and he always wanted to be with us.

Dad was a loving husband to our mom; a wonderful father to both of us and our wives; and an amazing grandfather to all our boys. When I first found out about my dad's cancer I was sad that my kids and my brother's kids wouldn't get a chance to grow up with this incredible Grandpa. My friend told me, "If they are going to know their grandfather, they have to see him in you guys. Today and every day."

LAST WEEK Ruby and I were blessed with a fourth grandson! Logan Matthew Price was born to our son, Matt, and his wife, Amy, and everyone is home and healthy. Thank You, God.

When I was first diagnosed with lung cancer we weren't sure if I would be alive to see Logan's birth. The Lord has granted me more days here on earth – not only so I could see this newborn's sweet face but, perhaps, be a godly influence in his life as he grows.

As much as my dad loved being a dad, I think he might have loved being Grandpa more. The boys thought he was the coolest grandpa ever. Dad knew he might not live to see the birth of his fifth grandson and that really grieved him. (He died three and a half months before Finly Jefferson Price was born to Matt and Amy, on August 1, 2011.)

He loved going to his grandsons' football games, gymnastic tournaments, baseball games and whatever other sport they were doing at the time. He always made it a priority to be at their sports, and they loved seeing Grammy and Grandpa in the stands.

Then there was the time in Hawaii when the boys got to jump around in the surf with Grandpa. On that same trip he even saved one of his grandsons from drowning when we were all snorkeling a little too far out in the ocean and were caught in a sudden blast of waves. Dad lost his very expensive snorkeling mask during the rescue operation, but said it was a "small price to pay."

My brother and I had a unique childhood - we basically grew up and lived at Canyonview Camp. Early memories include our dad playing worship songs on his guitar for countless singspirations in our home, while we ran and danced around the living room. Speaking of that living room, Dad loved getting down on the rug and wrestling with us or flipping us around. I'm pretty sure we were his exercise routine that kept him in shape for his Army physical-fitness tests!

Even though our dad was a gifted speaker and a wonderful teacher of the God's Word, his greatest gift to the world was the very personal way in which he related to people. Whatever my dad did and whomever he did it with, he was completely in the moment and gave them 100 percent of his attention. Dad's love for and relationships with people reflected how our heavenly Father relates to us. God used my dad's gift to change many lives and help guide people toward Christ.

Because God's love flowed freely through Dad, he could share God's limitless love with his family and with everyone. Dad overflowed with love and he was always there to hug us, guide us, and tell us he was proud of us. When I look at all the pictures he's in, I see love shining brightly in his eyes. The reason there was always love in his eyes (and his heart and his relationships) was because there was God in his life. Dad's love came from his love for and connection to Jesus Christ. In John 15:5, Jesus says:

"I AM THE VINE, YOU ARE THE BRANCHES; HE WHO ABIDES IN ME, AND I IN HIM, HE BEARS MUCH FRUIT; FOR APART FROM ME YOU CAN DO NOTHING."

One of the most effective and appreciated ways our dad communicated his love was by spending high-quality time with people. Our world is so hectic and people's schedules are so full, Dad's availability to those around him was a little shocking to some. Out of gratitude, because they knew he was super busy, people would say things like, "Dale always had time for me!"

People have said, "Your dad was the busiest person I know... who never talked about how busy he was!" This is so true! I rarely heard him talk about all the things he still needed to do.

Dad also lived a life of absolute integrity. Once he was under-charged 25 cents for a muffin and, more than a week later, he went back to the bakery and gave them the quarter he knew he owed them. We laughed about that but it was just one example of the commitment he had to living honestly.

*Dad loved God so much, he couldn't help sharing his Savior with others. In 2 Corinthians 5:14, the Apostle Paul says, "*THE LOVE OF CHRIST CONTROLS US.*" That love, Christ's love, certainly controlled him.*

Dad was not only an incredible father to us, he also served as a spiritual father to many others, including our wives, who he loved as his own daughters. More than a teacher, counselor, leader or mentor, our dad was a godly father for those who really needed one.

*I will choose, like my father, to have my life found in Christ. And I will choose to let the love of Christ control my life. Some day, when it's my time to leave this world, I will await these words from my heavenly Father - the same words that Dad heard on Saturday morning, April 16, 2011 - "*WELL DONE, MY GOOD AND FAITHFUL SERVANT.*"*

As much as my dad loved being a dad, I think he might have loved being Grandpa more. The boys thought he was the coolest grandpa ever.

Horizon

© *Matthew Price 2011*

My soul's worn out
It's just about
As thin as the soles of my shoes.
And this uphill path
In the shadow of death
Is sure not the one that I'd choose.

When the sun fades away
It's the light of your face that's guiding my way
Into your arms I run
When it's time to cross the horizon.

Once I felt so blessed
Lying on the grass
Beneath the clear blue sky.
But I never knew
How much I needed you
Until this cold rainy night

When the sun fades away
It's the light of your face that's guiding my way
Into your arms I run
When it's time to cross the horizon.

This might be a bitter pill to swallow,
But where you lead my I will follow
Where you lead my I will follow
Where you lead me I will follow

When the sun fades away
It's the light of your face that's guiding my way
Into your arms I run
When it's time to cross the horizon.
Into your arms I run
When it's time to cross the horizon.

Disciple by Elaine Roemen

Chapter 9

An Unending Story

"I asked God many times, 'OK, I can handle the cancer, even my death, but what about my family?' Eventually I came to believe that the Lord would take care of Ruby, the boys, and the rest of my family and do it even better than I could."

What makes a great book great? One answer is that the best books are the ones where you can't wait to find out what happens next. But, at the same time, you don't want to reach the book's final page. The story is so good you hope you'll never arrive at the end.

The story of Dale Price is that kind of story. But unlike any book or story you can get at amazon.com or your local library, Dale's story – since it is truly God's story, told through His servant, Dale – truly doesn't end. This, for those of us who knew and loved him, is a very good thing.

With the finish line in view

Two weeks before my dad's death my mom said, "Dad wants to write some final words of guidance to his sons and the grandkids." But the cancer was affecting his brain and he couldn't put his thoughts together into coherent sentences. She was devastated, but I told her that an end-of-life letter was unnecessary. He expressed his love so well and so frequently, we knew what was on his heart.

≈≈≈

Dale's primary focus was always Jesus and he never wavered in his faith. The song that comes to mind when I think about Dale's journey is "The Solid Rock." On Christ the solid rock I stand, all other ground is sinking sand. I sang this song to him on the last day of his life, when he couldn't respond and the Lord just gave me the words to whisper in his ear over the phone.

≈≈≈

Five days before he died, after a big day out in Seattle with the family, my dad and I talked late into the night as he was lying in bed. Thinking back on that time, I'm sure he knew he didn't have much more time left. That night there were many special things he told me about how to live my life as a man and husband, but the most important was to cherish my sons and help them develop a love for Jesus Christ.

It was hard for Ruby to watch Dale suffering and she told him, "It's OK, you can go now. It's OK." The final hours were special as the family did what they had done so often before. After the nurses let all nine family members crowd into the ICU, they all gathered around Dale and prayed, sang, played guitars and read the Bible to him, right up to the end.

When he died it was sad, of course, but it was also an amazing experience. Almost every person that had been involved with my dad's radiation treatments over the past two-and-a-half years came by to say good-bye while he was still conscious. As we were gathered around my dad at the hospital singing worship songs and reading the Bible, a doctor made the comment, "You can judge how a man lived his life by how much his family loves him."

Dale Ernest Price, 63, died April 16, 2011, with his family by his side in Seattle at Seattle Cancer Care Alliance, after a courageous battle with cancer. Just before he died, he awoke and took one last look at his family. One minute he was breathing, the next he was on his way home to be with his heavenly Father.

Like no one else I've ever met

When Dale first found out about his cancer, there was no pity. He knew that this was God's will and he accepted the challenge with the same gleam in his eyes as anything else. Dale and Ruby's faith was unaltered the whole time. His response really made me take a look at myself as far as where I was with my faith, my family, my friends and my work. I have made positive changes because of Dale and Ruby's influence in my life.

I am heartbroken that I have lost such a great friend and mentor, but I rejoice because I know that it will only be a short time until I can see him again in heaven. I thank God that he gave me the privilege of knowing Dale, Ruby and their family. I know that Ruby will continue to be a great friend and share her wisdom with me as well.

I hope that I can do half as good job as Dale and Ruby have done with their family, faith, love for each other, and sharing with others God's will.

ఌఌఌ

Over the past couple years I've noticed how Dale has worked hard to make sure everybody in his life is taken care of before he leaves. This reflects the heart of God, I believe; Jesus did the same thing when He was here, before He left those He loved.

ఌఌఌ

I ASKED God many times, "OK, I can handle the cancer, even my death, but what about my family?" Eventually I came to believe that the Lord would take care of Ruby, the boys and the rest of my family, and do it even better than I could.

We had the privilege of seeing Dale and Ruby in Oregon just a day after they returned from ministering in Russia. I know we all wondered if that would be the last time we would see each other. I will always remember Dale's words, "Don't worry about me. Follow through with what God has laid on your hearts to do. If we don't see each other again on earth, we will meet again in heaven." Indeed, just two months later, Dale passed into the Lord's presence.

⤨⤨⤨

We first met Dale in 1981 when we were searching for a site to hold a Christian camp for people with disabilities. Dale walked us through Canyonview Camp's very muddy and undeveloped grounds saying, "I'll share what I have with you." Though we ended up using a different location, he and I struck up a longtime friendship. The more I got to know Dale, the more I understood that he'd made a life and blessed a whole lot of folks by his sharing whatever he had.

My indelible image of Dale is seeing him welcome someone. Shoulders a little hunched forward, an arm outstretched and a big, open hand ready to shake hands or wrap you up in a hug. That smile, so big it seemed like it covered his face, and eyes that communicated, "you are important to me and to my God." Everyone got this special greeting from Dale; you didn't have to be someone important to get his attention. We praise God for providing us the opportunity to share in ministry together. His encouragement will always be in our ears.

The last time I saw him was at Canyonview Camp, giving pony rides and singing songs (many of which Dale wrote) with the kids. Dale hobbled up and greeted people, enjoying all of it immensely.

A social network in high-definition

Whether you love it or hate it, don't have an account or are logged in all day, Facebook is used by hundreds of millions the world over. Dozens of people visited Dale Price's Facebook page in the hours and days after his death. Friends, extended family, ministry partners and professional colleagues posted heartfelt tributes and comments, including these:

Your incredible teaching ability and your profound knowledge of Scripture is surpassed only by your deep love for the Lord, Ruby, your sons, and your grandsons. I just can't imagine a world without you in it, but I praise God for the healing you're enjoying now.

෧෧෧

"For me to live is Christ and to die is gain." Dale has gained what Paul wrote of and, by God's grace, I hope to do the same someday.

෧෧෧

Dale planted and nurtured Christ in me, and His Spirit in me lives on. I pray that I will be able to teach my daughter all Dale taught me, so she can abide in the One who holds everything in His hands.

∽⟨ô∿⟨ô∿⟨ô

*His energy and verve for life is something I have
never seen in another man. He saw in many the
light they could not see in themselves.*

*From the day you married us 29 years ago, you
have been a blessing and a spiritual rock in our
entire family.*

∽⟨ô∿⟨ô∿⟨ô

*I will miss you so much but am glad you're
already hanging with Jesus. It is hard to
imagine, but truly incredible at the same time.
Thank you for teaching me so much about God
– how to love, trust, and serve Him faithfully for
a lifetime, and do so with balance.*

∽⟨ô∿⟨ô∿⟨ô

*Dale, I'm sure you are having a blast dancing
with Jesus right now! You had a huge influence
on me when I was young, and even after I left
camp, your life has continued to inspire mine for
the better.*

∽⟨ô∿⟨ô∿⟨ô

*I miss you, Buzzard. Give Jesus a high-five for
me.*

∽⟨ô∿⟨ô∿⟨ô

*While your death puts a giant, gaping hole in
this world, there is a place in my heart that's
full of hope and light. Your life provided us with
beautiful examples of how God intended us to
love and serve.*

Shock and pain, but a sure and greater hope

I didn't expect so much pain, but the truth and reality of Dale's death showed me things I wasn't expecting. It shouldn't take someone's death to get our attention and show us that most all our stuff – religion, possessions, assumptions about who God is and what He values, etc. - is worthless. I was humbled when I realized this. I could never have imagined I would experience such pounding waves of grief.

∽ઝ∽ઝ∽ઝ

Dale's battle with cancer brought into clearer view the reliance we must have on Christ. It is His finished work on the cross that gives us peace and security, not our circumstances. Christ's blood gives us confidence, so we can stand blameless before God. Even though Dale worked tirelessly for the Lord, his only hope was in Jesus.

The message of Dale's life is what God did, not what Dale did. We are amazed by all Dale did, but what counted was his faithfulness in allowing God to work through him.

∽ઝ∽ઝ∽ઝ

Dale and Ruby have produced an incredible legacy. Their lives testify to me and everyone about their faith and trust in the living God, our faithful refuge and the lover of our souls.

God rewarded Dale's faithfulness and goodness with greater leadership responsibility; access to the joy of his God and Savior; and an abundance of spiritual riches.

The days ahead

The death of a loved one, especially one as loved as Dale, often produces reflection in people that results in changed lives. The principle found in 1 Corinthians 15:36 ("THAT WHICH YOU SOW DOES NOT COME TO LIFE UNLESS IT DIES") and the death and resurrection of Christ remind us that new life often requires the death of another.

> *Dale's passing is a wakeup call for everyone. I've become keenly aware of how short life is and what we need to be concerned with.*

ॐॐॐ

> *Because of what's happened with Dale and Ruby, I'm starting to realize that every day is precious. I need to live in the present, not the past of the future. Following their example, I want to tell my kids about Jesus and encourage them to live completely for Him. I want a stronger relationship with God and more time in the Word. The Prices obviously made their marriage a top priority and so will I.*

Dale clung to God's Word, loving it and living out the truth in it to the very last moment. He was so comforted by abiding in Christ and letting the Word of God minister life and encouragement to him and Ruby. God did a beauti- ful work of transforming Dale, His obedient servant, into the image of Christ over the years.

⊰⊰⊰

After Dale died I asked myself, "Why didn't you ask more fervently for his healing?" And I began examining my prayer life in light of that question. I started changing how I prayed, going to God with confidence and pouring out everything that was on my heart. Asking boldly for healing and miracles and divine interventions.

⊰⊰⊰

Dale's death quieted me down and helped me start really listening to God. I wanted the kind of relationship Dale and Ruby had with God. These days I'm asking Him, "Where do I need to spend my time? What's Your purpose in my life?"

I HAVE come to realize in all of these things that our comprehension of our time on earth is an illusion. The moment in which we live is all we have and it is where God's will is realized. It is in the present, now, that we learn to abide, to trust, to hope, to love, to be filled with His peace and joy.

My heart is filled with compassion for you, Ruby. Dale was a wonderful man and the two of you made an amazing team! I pray that you will feel the freedom to grieve wholly and completely, and be able to do so in your own timeframe. I pray that you will find solace in being with your family and friends; that writing, talking, and sharing will be cathartic; and that what you're learning in the present will develop into something that allows you to share the love of Jesus.

⊰⊰⊰

Grief is uncomfortable for those who walk outside of it. They want to fix it or help us try to remove it. But the grieving is where God meets us, loves on us and, in time, brings about His plans for us.

I'm praying for your peace. Not the absence of pain or conflict, but the peace that arrives in the person of Jesus Christ, alive in you. Thank you, Ruby, for being transparent, vulnerable, honest, and in motion. You're not stuck in the past or striving for the future, but living in the (painful) present, willing to share what you're experiencing so others can benefit. You are a super hero, not because you are "beating this thing" but because you are walking through it.

A new and continuing journey

It's not surprising that the No. 1 question that's asked following a death is, "How is she/he doing?" For Ruby Price, answering that question has often been impossible. She continues in the path she and God began in her youth, the path that intensified after her marriage to Dale. But, there are no easy answers, no quick fixes. What Ruby does know for sure is that her Lord will provide what she needs for the road ahead.

June 1, 2011

To my beloved children,

Jennifer and Amy, you are dear daughters to Dale and me. Josh and Matt, you are my dear sons. You blessed him beyond measure by letting him be "Dad" to you. He was so proud of you all; he would be even more proud if he could see how you've been over the past few weeks. I am speaking from my heart of hearts, which has been stabbed by grief.

I was thankful to have the time for our family grief-counseling session with Pastor Ben. As you know, as I prepared for it by searching for Dad's cards and writings over our lifetime, I began to weep well before I arrived. Once the tears start to flow, they are so hard to turn off.

There was much more I wanted to say to you; I don't know if I can say what I want to say in person, so I am writing it down.

When I got home, I kept hearing in my mind what I said to Pastor Ben, "I don't want to do life without Dale." That statement was a mistake. I know now it was the ugly grief monster speaking, that which is trying to strangle the life out of me.

What I meant to say was, "I don't know how to live life without Dad." I also meant to say, "I don't know how to live without your dad." I cry so much, and I don't know how not to cry right now. I have never gone through this level of pain before. We have never been challenged in this way, individually or as a family. One thing is certain, though: I love you from the depth of my heart of hearts. You and our precious grandsons are such comfort to me, as you were to Dad and me together.

You have been a blessing to me, particularly as we have walked through Dad's prolonged illness and death. Thank you for trying to understand me during this time of ongoing, profound sorrow and transition. How we navigate today will impact our lives tomorrow.

After 41 years of living with Dale, my brain doesn't understand what life is like without him. The despair of missing him is with me every moment. Yet none of us can fill that void, nor is it even appropriate for us to consider doing so.

I loved him with all my heart as I know you did. You are the mothers and fathers of his beloved grandsons and he was so thankful that his grandchildren have parents who love them so much. You were precious to him beyond compare, and he spoke of you with love that transcends time.

Yes, our Savior Jesus Christ, to whom your father dedicated his strength, love, and enduring devotion, will carry me with your assistance to the new life and understandings we all long for and are incapable of creating by ourselves.

As we move forward in our tenuous steps into a new life without Dad, we will re-establish a sense of family without our precious leader. We will learn together how to do our new life, you without your father and me as a grieving widow. In my pain my Savior talks to me daily. He is acquainted with grief and knows profound sorrow. He will lead us, like Abraham, into our new land.

With full devotion,

Mom

Ruby's personal grief journal – July 2011

In "A Grief Observed," C.S. Lewis' account of his grieving after his wife died from cancer, Lewis said, "I not only am living each endless day in grief, but live each day thinking about living each day in grief. But what am I to do?" He's right. What am I supposed to do, now that Dale is gone?

It became clear to me that like C.S. Lewis, who also said "Perhaps the bereaved ought to be isolated in special settlements like lepers," I needed a place of personal retreat to help me more completely experience the disabling grief I'm in following the death of my husband. That, indeed, is what I have done.

The following thoughts come from endless reading (especially of grief literature), walking (in rain and sun), calling out to my beloved husband when sleep won't come, and praying/groaning with the help of the Spirit.

During this time away, I continue to count my blessings to be married to Dale. Daily he demonstrated incredible courage as he confronted the powerful uncertainty of his mortality.

I have been reading and re-reading a tattered piece of paper on which Dale wrote,

"I **HAVE** come to realize in all of these things that our comprehension of our time on earth is an illusion. The moment in which we live is all we have and it is where God's will is realized. It is in the present now that we learn to abide, to trust, to hope, to love, to be filled with His peace and joy. I pray that you will find God's perfect peace as you abide in His love. It is the only place where I have found joy in the midst of what may be terminal for me. We may all be Home sooner than expected."

Throughout our nearly three-year walk with cancer, Dale and I found that looking back could bring regrets and looking forward, fear. The only place where we could find peace and joy was in the present. In fact, we were so busy living in the present that when Dale was taken so quickly I was shocked and totally unprepared.

Someone has said that the death of a beloved spouse is an amputation. I agree. The reason "amputation" is such an apt description is because, in marriage, two people become one flesh. The amputation that took place on April 16, 2011, severed and removed an essential part of me. No wonder my wounds are bleeding so profusely and need to be bound up. Eventually, I hope, they will be healed, too.

Some people are waiting for – even urging – me to "get over" Dale's death and "move on." These comments may be delivered with the intent to support me, but they don't. My response is sometimes anger, sometimes frustration, but I'm always challenged to think about my grieving process.

Usually, however, I find these attitudes shocking. To think I could "get over" a man like Dale is crazy; I never want to "get over" him – he's my husband! How can the duration (not to mention the intensity) of one's grief be measured or scheduled?

When we lose someone we love, we experience many losses, not just one. There are physical losses, symbolic losses, present-day losses, and the loss of what we thought we would have in the future. All these losses must be recognized and worked through.

As I take time to examine my grief, I'm surprised and shocked by its intensity. I also understand that grief is not just the prerogative of those who have recently lost a loved one. Grief is a constant for the wife who must watch her life partner and beloved husband gradually succumb to a terminal illness. Yes, I am referring to the 32 months I journeyed with Dale through his cancer.

Right now I am overwhelmed as I dissect each decision, wondering if only we had taken another path, would he be here with me now?

Grief doesn't stand still, nor is it like a book you can put down and pick up at another time of your choosing. Grief also doesn't come pre-packaged in neat stages to be experienced in sequence. There are many different emotions over time. During this time of acute grieving, one description of my grief is the feeling of powerful waves crashing over me as I drown in emotional pain and yearning. Then, there are the times when I am almost fine (for a moment) and then quickly and wrenchingly become a puddle of tears and distress, spread out all over the floor.

Despite all this grief, God brought us great joy in the form of our fifth grandson, Finly Jefferson Price. He was born to Matt (our younger son) and his wonderful wife, Amy, on August 1, 2011. Dale didn't live to see his newest grandson, but as I told him at his grave (just a mile from the hospital where Finly was born), "He is our comfort and your legacy."

Grieving is not a completely private experience/activity, and the ways people react to another's grief can vary widely. As Meghan O'Rourke said in a February 2011 article in the New York Times, "Most people are uncomfortable around loss. Friends talk to you about 'getting through it' and 'moving on' and 'healing.' No one wants to say the wrong thing." And many choose to say nothing, which can be very frustrating for the person grieving.

In the same article, Joyce Carol Oates says, "There is a strange sort of expectation that grief should conform to a general pattern of principle. There are even scientific polls measuring what is 'normal' and 'extreme grief. As if individuals are not radically different, and grief will not manifest itself differently in different individuals! Profound losses leave us paralyzed and mute, unable really to comprehend them, still less to speak coherently about them."

I'm grateful to my family and a few close friends who are helping me, being strong when I'm not.

Thank you for the many blessings you have extended to me. You have been my rock and foundation as we have traversed the treacherous waters of Dale's death. I could not have survived these past days or contemplated the future without knowing that you have been and will be there for me. These past few days you have comforted me

"I have come to realize in all of these things that our comprehension of our time on earth is an illusion. The moment in which we live is all we have and it is where God's will is realized. It is in the present, now, that we learn to abide, to trust, to hope, to love, to be filled with His peace and joy."

beyond words.

You were prayer warriors with us as we prayed for a miracle, that Dale would be healed. But gradually we began to realize and understand that we were living in the midst of the miracle! Dale courageously and transparently demonstrated to us all how to live life triumphantly under great adversity. He never complained while enduring almost nonstop pain, especially in recent months. He didn't waste his pain, but let God use it to minister to hurting people all around him.

It's very hard to pray right now. The Word is precious and I have favorite passages that help sustain me.

I'm giving myself permission not to try and be super-spiritual or do the "Christian" thing a lot of people expect a widow to do. I know that even when I'm not praying, others are.

Love, Ruby

Remembering and celebrating

Dale Price's memorial service was held at Canyonview Camp on Saturday, April 23, 2011. Hundreds attended to honor his life, his faith and his legacy.

As I planned the service I spent lots of time in Scripture, thinking about Dad and his life, what he meant to me and others. I asked myself, What would Dad want us to say at the service?

I invited people to stand if they felt that in some way Dad had been a spiritual father to them, and dozens stood up. Then I asked, "If you felt that your relationship with my dad was more than that of a friend, similar to the family bond shared between a brother AND sister, please stand up." Dozens more rose to their feet.

By then, more than 100 people were standing! This tribute to my dad's part in people's lives was a visual representation of what I always knew to be true of Dad. He poured his life into people. He loved everyone - family, neighbors, friends and strangers. Those of us who have been lucky enough to be loved by him know how blessed we are.

᪥᪥᪥

Dale's memorial service was a very honorable tribute to his life and ministry, but I walked away feeling that one element was missing. Nothing was mentioned of his last 18 months in Creswell. Nothing was said about Ruby's life as an educator and Dale's strategic decision to move from the camp to Creswell, where he would give his final months to supporting her in the calling God had put on her heart. While much was said of Dale's deep love for Ruby, nothing was said of his choice to go with her to Creswell, to step into her shadow, to love her "as Jesus loved the church."

This, I believe, is a huge part of who Dale Price had become, as a man and as a husband. This is a message I believe Dale would have wanted to communicate – to his sons especially, and to every man whose life has been touched by Dale's. This is the most profound message Dale Price communicated to me – partly in words, mostly by his actions. It is this that I will most remember about Dale.

༺ஃ༻ஃ༺ஃ༻

Dad's legacy is not about what we say at this memorial today. It's about what we do tomorrow, and the next day, and for the rest of our lives. Who is hurting and needs our help? Who do we know that needs Christ's love, but we haven't shared and showed that love yet? To whom will we open our homes? How will we raise our children in the confident love of Christ? Into whom can we pour our lives?

In 1 Corinthians 11:1, the Apostle Paul says, "BE IMITATORS OF ME AS I AM OF CHRIST." Today, I urge every one of us to be imitators of my dad, because he was an imitator of Christ.

༺ஃ༻ஃ༺ஃ༻

We don't ever "get over" losing a loved one. We simply get through the different anniversaries, milestones, and adjustments with God's grace and mercy. May He continue to show Himself faithful in and through the grieving and bring joy in the morning and the mourning.

Epilogue

Dale Price "crossed the horizon" in the early hours of April 16th, 2011. Even as he and his wife of 41 years headed back to Seattle on April 3rd for another round of whole brain radiation, he didn't say goodbye to anyone; he was prepared to keep fighting.

He loved the life the Lord gave him. He once told me, "Next to cuddling with my wife and grandsons, my favorite thing to do is teaching the Gospel." He desired to do much more cuddling and much more teaching. Dale leaves behind his beloved wife Ruby, son and daughter-in-law Josh and Jennifer Price and their sons Tyler and Cody, son and daughter-in-law Matt and Amy Price and their sons Noah, Logan, and Finly.

I would end this book with "WELL DONE, GOOD AND FAITHFUL SERVANT" (MATTHEW 25:21). Dale would end it with "I AM AN UNWORTHY SLAVE; I HAVE DONE ONLY THAT WHICH I OUGHT TO HAVE DONE" (LUKE 17:10).

Jaira Hill

Made in the USA
Charleston, SC
26 November 2011